The 48 Laws of Inner and Outer Righteous Power

How Identity, Discipline, and Strategy Shape Destiny

Azrael Sidiiq

Afrodescendant Solutions

This work is intended for educational, historical, and cultural enrichment. References to historical figures, public events, and institutions are presented for research, commentary, and discussion.

Publisher

Afrodescendant Solutions

An Independent Publishing Imprint of Afrodescendant Branded LLC

Afrodescendant Solutions is dedicated to producing works that advance education, historical understanding, cultural identity, and intellectual empowerment throughout the Afrodescendant world.

Edition Information

First Edition

Printed in the United States of America

Bibliographic Information

ISBN: 978-1-972094-04-4

(Paperback)

Distribution Notice

This book is independently published and distributed globally through major book retail and distribution platforms including Amazon.

Contact

Afrodescendant Solutions Publishing

Email: AfrodescendantSolutions@Gmail.com

For bulk orders, speaking engagements, educational partnerships, or licensing inquiries, contact the publisher directly.

Mission Statement

Afrodescendant Solutions exists to preserve knowledge, elevate truth, and empower communities through literature, research, and creative expression. Our publications seek to contribute to a broader understanding of history, identity, and human potential.

To those who refused to accept
the identity the world attempted to assign them.
To those who chose discipline over chaos,
strategy over reaction,
and purpose over distraction.
And to every individual and community
determined to define their own future
rather than inherit someone else's definition.
May this work serve as both
a compass and a shield
on the journey toward clarity, dignity,
and self-determined power.

EPIGRAPH PAGE

"Power concedes nothing without a demand.
It never did and it never will."
— Frederick Douglass
"The most powerful weapon in the hands of the oppressor
is the mind of the oppressed."
— Steve Biko
"He who knows himself is wise;
he who governs himself is powerful."
— Lao Tzu

Table of Contents

True authority does not shout.

Law 7 — Guard Your Energy Like a Strategic Resource

Power leaks through distraction.

Law 8 — Control Emotional Signals Before Others Use Them

Your reactions reveal leverage.

PART II — THE ARCHITECTURE OF INFLUENCE

How Authority and Credibility Are Built

Here the reader learns how influence actually works in human environments.

Law 9 — Study the System Before Moving Within It

Observation precedes strategy.

Law 10 — Position Yourself Where Opportunity Must Pass You

Placement multiplies effort.

Law 11 — Become Valuable Enough That You Cannot Be Ignored

Indispensability builds authority.

Law 12 — Control Access to Yourself to Increase Your Value

Scarcity creates perceived importance.

Law 13 — Shape Your Reputation Before Others Shape It

Your name is strategic currency.

Law 14 — Align With Power Without Losing Yourself

Association opens doors.

Law 15 — Make Others Feel Powerful in Your Presence

Influence grows when egos feel safe.

Law 16 — Convert Conflict Into Leverage

Opposition can become advantage.

PART III — STRATEGIC NAVIGATION

Understanding Systems, Incentives, and Hidden Rules

This section teaches the reader how power moves inside institutions.

Law 17 — Study Incentives Before Trusting Words

Contents

HOW TO USE THIS BOOK

This book is not meant to be read once and forgotten.

It is designed as a strategic manual.

The 48 Laws presented here are tools, principles that help individuals understand power, identity, discipline, and long-term strategy in a complex world.

You may approach this book in several ways:

Read Sequentially

Reading the laws in order provides a structured framework.

The book moves from personal mastery to system awareness, then to social strategy, economic power, and finally long-term leadership habits.

Study Individual Laws

Each law stands on its own.

Readers may return to specific chapters whenever they face challenges requiring clarity or strategic thinking.

Reflect and Apply

Every chapter concludes with a Strategic Training Drill.

These exercises are designed to help translate ideas into action.

Powerful principles become meaningful only when they are practiced consistently.

Return Often

Like any manual of strategy, this book gains value through repetition.

Each reading reveals new insights as your experience and perspective evolve.

Ultimately, the purpose of this book is not simply to inform.

It is to encourage readers to think carefully about their identity, their environment, and the systems that shape opportunity.

Because the greatest power anyone can develop is the ability to understand their circumstances clearly and act with intention.

Introduction

INTRODUCTION

The System You Cannot See

There are systems in this world that do not announce themselves.

They do not wear uniforms.

They do not march in formation.

They do not shout their intentions.

They operate quietly, in policies, in patterns, in data, in algorithms, in institutional habits, in cultural narratives, in economic structures, and in the subconscious expectations of society.

And the most sophisticated systems are the ones whose participants do not even realize they are operating inside of them.

This book is about navigating that reality.

It is about understanding that modern power is no longer only visible in laws and physical barriers. It now exists in subtle code, in who gets called back for interviews, in who is labeled "aggressive" versus "assertive," in how neighborhoods are valued, in how schools are funded, in how digital platforms amplify or suppress voices, in how reputations are quietly shaped, and in how identities are framed long before individuals speak for themselves.

The modern machine is not always loud.

It is efficient.

It is data-driven.

It is pattern-based.

And it often "appears" neutral.

But neutrality in a system built upon historical imbalance does not produce fairness. It produces refinement.

Refined bias.

Refined exclusion.

Refined programming.

This book does not exist to promote anger.

It does not exist to promote victimhood.

It does not exist to promote hostility.

It exists to promote power.

Not domination.

Not manipulation.

Not ego.

Power, in its righteous and disciplined form.

Power that begins internally.

Power that expresses strategically.

Power that does not beg.

Power that does not overreact.

Power that understands the terrain before making a move.

For generations, so called Black Americans have navigated systems that were not built with them in mind. Some systems were explicitly hostile. Others were quietly indifferent. Today's systems are often more complex. They are structured through technology, corporate policies, financial instruments, academic filters, social perception algorithms, and digital reputation metrics.

To fight a visible enemy requires courage.

To navigate an invisible one requires intelligence.

The purpose of this book is not to teach you how to "fight the system" emotionally.

It is to teach you how to understand it, anticipate it, maneuver within it, build outside of it, and, when necessary, redefine yourself beyond it.

There are two wars every serious person must master.

The inner war.

And the outer war.

The inner war is about programming.

What beliefs were installed in you before you had the "language" to question them?

What emotional triggers were conditioned into you?

What labels were attached to you?

What narratives did you inherit?

If your internal software is compromised, no external strategy will save you.

The outer war is about structure.

How do institutions operate?

How do corporations think?

How do algorithms categorize?

How does bias disguise itself as policy?

How does "professionalism" get defined?

How does power quietly replicate itself?

If you do not understand the structure, you will mistake outcomes for accidents.

This book operates on both levels.

It recognizes that modern racism, when it exists, is rarely crude. It is coded. It is procedural. It is statistical. It is algorithmic. It hides inside systems that claim objectivity. It hides inside data models. It hides inside hiring matrices. It hides inside funding pipelines. It hides inside language itself.

But here is the greater truth.

Systems, no matter how sophisticated, still rely on human psychology.

And psychology can be "mastered".

Institutions, no matter how powerful, still rely on predictable patterns.

And patterns can be studied.

Algorithms, no matter how complex, still reflect the assumptions of those who built them.

And assumptions can be decoded.

This book gives you 48 laws, not to dominate others, but to prevent domination. Not to manipulate, but to avoid manipulation. Not to inflame, but to stabilize.

Each law works on multiple levels.

Personal level. Professional level. Economic level. Digital level. Relational level. Collective level.

You will learn how to, Reclaim identity before it is assigned.

Control your digital footprint before it defines you.

Anticipate bias before it appears.

Separate emotion from strategy.

Build insulation in hostile environments.

Protect your reputation like sovereign territory.

Read subtext in conversations and policies.

Use documentation as armor.

Think in decades, not moments.

Develop parallel paths instead of waiting for permission.

You will also learn something deeper.

True power is not loud.

True power is measured.

True power is disciplined.

True power is strategic.

And the highest form of power is self-determination.

Not as a slogan.

But as a practice.

The practice of defining who you are, what you stand for, how you move, how you build, how you respond, and how you position yourself in systems that may not have anticipated your success.

This book is not about rage.

It is about readiness.

It is not about blame.

It is about blueprint.

It is not about rebellion without structure.

It is about structure that makes rebellion unnecessary.

There are readers who will approach this book seeking confirmation of frustration.

They will not find it.

There are readers who will approach this book seeking shortcuts.

They will not find those either.

What they will find is discipline.

Clarity.

Strategy.

And a recalibration of how power truly works in modern America.

If you master the inner war, you cannot be psychologically broken.

If you master the outer war, you cannot be easily outmaneuvered.

If you master both, you become something rare.

A person who understands the system without being consumed by it.

A person who can operate within structures while quietly building beyond them.

A person who knows when to speak and when to observe.

A person who cannot be programmed without consent.

That is inner and outer power.

That is the purpose of this book.

Let us begin.

Chapter One

Law I Know Who You Are Before They Tell You Who You Are

There is a truth about modern power that most people discover too late. Long before you enter a room, the room has already formed an opinion about you. In today's world, classification precedes conversation. You are assessed before you speak, interpreted before you act, and placed into mental categories before you introduce yourself. Systems, corporate, educational, digital, and social, do not begin with opportunity; they begin with interpretation. They measure race, background, language, tone, dress, associations, digital presence, and dozens of subtle signals that most people do not even realize are being scanned. The outcome of that interpretation may not be immediate, but the frame is already set.

"This is why identity is the first battlefield".

If you do not know who you are before entering that system, you will unconsciously absorb the definitions it assigns to you. And once you accept a definition, you accept the limits attached to it. You may not even recognize it happening. You might hesitate before speaking. You might overexplain your credentials. You might shrink in certain environments or overcompensate in others. You might tolerate subtle disrespect because part of you believes you are fortunate to be included. None of this is accidental. It is psychological architecture shaped over time.

Modern systems rarely operate through obvious hostility. They operate through expectation. Expectation shapes perception. Perception shapes behavior. Behavior shapes outcome. Outcome reinforces stereotype. And the cycle quietly continues. The most powerful systems do not need to openly suppress you if you have already internalized a ceiling.

That is why the most dangerous labels are the ones that feel normal. Words like "minority," "underrepresented," "at-risk," "urban," "diversity hire," or even "articulate" carry hidden assumptions. They may appear neutral or even complimentary, yet they subtly define parameters. When repeated enough, they begin to inform how you see yourself. And when you see yourself through a constrained lens, you move accordingly.

This law requires a personal audit.

Who told you who you were? Was it media narratives? Educational systems? Corporate culture? Historical distortions? Family survival instincts? Statistical generalizations? Which parts of your identity are self-defined, and which were inherited without examination? If your internal narrative is second-hand, your strategy will be second-hand as well.

Knowing who you are is not arrogance. It is stability. Arrogance is fragile and reactive. Grounded identity is disciplined and deliberate. When you know who you are, you do not search the room for approval. You do not perform for validation. You do not shrink to avoid discomfort. You operate from clarity. And clarity alters posture, tone, negotiation stance, boundaries, and expectation.

The system relies on confusion. A confused identity is predictable. A predictable identity is manageable. A manageable identity is controllable. But a grounded identity introduces uncertainty into the equation. It becomes harder to manipulate someone who has already defined themselves.

This does not mean ignoring reality. It means refusing to internalize limitation. There is a difference. You can understand structural bias without allowing it to define your worth. You can anticipate perception without being ruled by it. You can navigate difficult terrain without surrendering your internal ground.

Before you enter any space, professional, academic, digital, or social, pause and ask yourself: What assumptions may already exist about me? What identity have I unconsciously accepted? Where do I shrink? Where do I overcompensate? Where am I reacting instead of operating?

Then recalibrate. Bring your definition with you. Bring your expectations with you. Bring your boundaries with you. When you define yourself first, you remove the system's ability to define you by default.

Inner power always precedes outer power.

If you do not control your identity, your identity will control you. And if your identity is shaped by a system that was not designed with your full humanity in mind, your power will always be conditional.

Know who you are before they tell you who you are.

Everything else begins there.

Chapter Two

Law 2 Reprogram Your Mind Before the System Programs It for You

Most people believe they are thinking for themselves.

They are not.

They are thinking with language they inherited, reacting with emotions they were conditioned to feel, and making decisions shaped by beliefs they never consciously chose. This is not an insult. It is a condition of human development. Every person enters the world with a mind that must be taught how to interpret reality. Families teach. Schools teach. Media teaches. Culture teaches. Experience teaches.

Even silence teaches. Long before a person is old enough to question anything, patterns of interpretation are already installed.

This process is programming.

Programming is not always malicious. It is simply the process through which the mind learns what things mean. But here is where power enters the conversation: if you do not consciously choose your programming, someone or something else will choose it for you. And whatever programs you inherit will quietly govern how you see yourself, how you see opportunity, how you see authority, and how you see possibility.

Most people assume oppression must be loud to be real. In truth, the most effective form of control is subtle. It does not announce itself as control. It presents itself as normal. It appears as common sense. It sounds like advice. It looks like tradition. It feels like realism. Yet beneath that appearance may exist assumptions that were never designed for your growth.

The modern system does not need to tell you directly that you cannot succeed. It only needs to surround you with enough signals that you begin to question whether you can. It does not need to forbid ambition. It only needs to make ambition feel unrealistic. It does not need to block your path. It only needs to convince you the path is not meant for you.

This is psychological programming at its most refined.

If a person grows up repeatedly exposed to narratives that portray them as behind, limited, threatening, less capable, or perpetually struggling, those images begin to form a subconscious script. That script may operate quietly for years, influencing decisions without announcing itself. A person might hesitate to apply for an opportunity, not because they lack ability, but because something inside them whispers that they do not belong. Another may overwork themselves to exhaustion, not because excellence demands it, but because they feel they must prove they deserve to exist in a space. Another may downplay their intelligence to avoid being perceived as intimidating. These reactions feel personal, yet they often originate from inherited programming.

The danger of unconscious programming is not that it exists. The danger is that it operates without your permission.

Reprogramming the mind does not mean rejecting everything you were taught. It means examining it. It means asking, "Who installed this belief? Does it serve me? Does it limit me? Is it accurate? Is it outdated? Is it rooted in truth or repetition?" Questions are tools of liberation because they interrupt automatic thinking. Automatic thinking is efficient, but it is also easy to control. Conscious thinking requires effort, but it restores authorship over your life.

Every sophisticated system understands the importance of mental framing. Institutions train employees. Militaries train soldiers. Corporations train executives. Nations train citizens. Training exists because whoever controls interpretation controls response. If interpretation can be shaped, behavior can be predicted. And if behavior can be predicted, outcomes can be managed.

This is why mental discipline is not optional for anyone seeking power. It is foundational. A disciplined mind does not accept every narrative it hears. It examines. It filters. It compares. It tests. It verifies. It refuses to let repetition replace truth.

Reprogramming your mind requires deliberate practice. It requires exposure to knowledge that expands your perspective rather than shrinks it. It requires replacing internal language that weakens you with language that strengthens you. It requires observing your reactions and asking whether they are chosen or conditioned. It requires recognizing that many limitations are psychological long before they are structural.

None of this happens accidentally.

The default mind reflects its environment. The trained mind reshapes it.

This law is not about denial. It is about authorship. You are not pretending systems do not exist. You are refusing to let systems dictate your internal software. You may not control every external structure, but you always retain authority over how your mind interprets reality. That authority is one of the greatest powers any person can possess.

When your mind is programmed by others, you react.

When your mind is programmed by you, you decide.

The difference between reaction and decision is the difference between being managed and being self-directed.

Before you attempt to change your environment, examine your mental framework. Before you attempt to correct the world, correct your interpretation of it. Before you attempt to build external power, secure internal sovereignty.

Because the person who masters their own mind cannot be easily controlled by any system.

Reprogram your mind before the system programs it for you.

Principle of Law 2

Whoever controls your thinking controls your direction.

If you do not choose your mental framework, one will be chosen for you.

Chapter Three

Law 3 Master Silence, Power Moves Loudly Announced Lose Their Force

There is a difference between having power and appearing powerful. Many people confuse the two, and in doing so they unintentionally weaken themselves. True power is rarely noisy. It does not rush to announce itself, justify itself, or display itself. Instead, it observes, listens, calculates, and moves with precision. Silence is not absence. Silence is discipline. Silence is control. Silence is strategy.

The undisciplined mind feels compelled to speak. It wants to explain its intentions, declare its plans, defend its position, and narrate its thoughts as they form. This urge feels natural, even harmless. Yet every unnecessary word reveals information, and information is leverage. When you speak impulsively, you expose timing, emotion, uncertainty, and motive. A trained observer can learn more from what you say than you realize you are revealing. For this reason, silence has always been one of the most underestimated instruments of influence.

Silence does not mean passivity. It means deliberate restraint. It means choosing speech instead of reacting with speech. The silent person is not inactive; they are gathering data. While others fill space with noise, they are studying patterns. They are noticing inconsistencies. They are identifying alliances. They are measuring intentions. They are mapping the terrain. Silence turns observation into intelligence, and intelligence into advantage.

Most people speak to be seen. The strategic person watches to understand.

In competitive environments, those who talk the most are often the easiest to predict. They reveal what they want, what they fear, and what they intend to do. Predictability reduces power. When others can anticipate your move, they can prepare for it. They can counter it. They can neutralize it. But when your intentions are not prematurely revealed, you retain initiative. Initiative is one of the highest forms of advantage because it allows you to choose timing. Timing, more than force, determines outcomes.

Silence also protects you from emotional exposure. Words spoken in anger, insecurity, pride, or frustration often reveal vulnerabilities that would have otherwise remained hidden. Many conflicts escalate not because of actions, but because of statements made without restraint. A single careless sentence can undo years of trust, credibility, or authority. Silence, in these moments, acts as a shield. It prevents temporary emotion from producing permanent consequence.

There is another dimension to silence that few recognize: silence commands attention. When someone speaks constantly, listeners eventually tune them out. But when a person speaks rarely and deliberately, people lean in when they do speak. Their words carry weight because they are not wasted. The less frequently you speak, the more value your speech appears to hold. Authority is often perceived not by volume, but by restraint.

Consider the environments where the highest stakes decisions are made. Skilled negotiators listen more than they talk. Effective leaders speak last, not first. Master strategists ask questions rather than make declarations. They understand that information gathered quietly is more valuable than attention gained loudly. Attention is fleeting. Information is actionable.

Silence also disrupts manipulation. Many manipulative tactics depend on provoking a reaction. They rely on drawing you into arguments, triggering defensiveness, or forcing you to reveal your position prematurely. When you refuse to react immediately, the manipulator loses control of the exchange. Silence denies them feedback. Without feedback, they cannot calibrate their approach. Without calibration, their influence weakens.

This is why disciplined silence can feel unsettling to others. People expect predictable reactions. When you respond with composure instead of impulse, you introduce uncertainty into their calculations. Uncertainty shifts the balance of control. The person who cannot read you cannot easily control you.

Silence also strengthens internal power. When you learn to pause before speaking, you train your mind to evaluate rather than react. This strengthens judgment. It increases awareness. It sharpens perception. Over time, the habit of measured response replaces impulsive reaction. What begins as restraint becomes mastery.

Mastery of silence is not about refusing to speak. It is about choosing when speech is useful. Speak when words will move something forward. Speak when clarity is required. Speak when direction must be set. Speak when truth must be established. But never speak merely because the moment feels empty. Empty moments are not problems to be filled. They are opportunities to observe.

In a world saturated with noise, the person who can remain composed in silence possesses a rare advantage. They cannot be easily rushed. They cannot be easily baited. They cannot be easily decoded. Their stillness becomes presence. Their restraint becomes authority. Their words, when spoken, become decisive.

Power that announces itself invites resistance.

Power that moves quietly often arrives uncontested.

Principle of Law 3

Silence is not weakness. Silence is stored strength.

The one who speaks less sees more, learns more, and controls more.

Strategic Training Drill, Law 3

Practice the discipline of silence daily:

In conversation, let others finish fully before responding.

When provoked, pause three seconds before speaking.

Ask one question before offering one opinion.

Observe body language before interpreting words.

Speak only when your words improve the situation.

Master this, and you will begin to notice something most never see:

Those who rush to speak are often led.

Those who master silence are often followed.

Chapter Four

Law 4 Control Perception Before Others Define You

Before people decide how to treat you, they decide what you are.

They may never say it out loud. They may not even realize they are doing it. But within seconds of encountering you, the human mind begins forming conclusions. It categorizes. It labels. It assigns value. This process is automatic. It is not always fair, not always accurate, and not always conscious, but it is constant. Perception is the first battlefield of power, and whoever establishes it first often determines how every interaction that follows will unfold.

Many people attempt to prove themselves through effort alone. They work harder, speak louder, or try repeatedly to demonstrate their worth after they have already been underestimated. This approach exhausts energy because it fights against an established perception rather than shaping it from the beginning. Once someone has placed you into a mental category, they unconsciously interpret your actions through that label. Evidence that supports their assumption is noticed. Evidence that contradicts it is ignored. This is not malice. It is psychology.

Because perception filters reality, controlling perception is one of the most efficient forms of influence.

This does not mean deception. It means intentional presentation. It means deciding what aspects of yourself are visible first, what tone you set when entering a room, how you speak, how you move, how you carry your posture, and what signals you send before you ever explain anything. People rarely meet your full reality immediately. They meet your presentation. Presentation becomes interpretation, and interpretation becomes treatment.

Those who understand power do not wait for perception to form randomly. They construct it deliberately.

Consider how institutions establish authority. They do not rely solely on their function. They design symbols, language, uniforms, architecture, and ceremony. These elements are not accidental. They communicate credibility before a word is spoken. A person entering such an environment often feels the authority of the institution before any rule is enforced. The perception creates the experience.

Individuals can apply the same principle.

If you enter spaces uncertain, apologetic, or hesitant, others may unconsciously mirror that uncertainty back to you. But when you enter with composure, clarity, and presence, people often adjust their behavior accordingly. Humans continuously read signals from one another. We interpret confidence, hesitation, tension, calmness, certainty, and doubt through subtle cues. Your posture speaks. Your eye contact speaks. Your tone speaks. Your timing speaks. Silence speaks. Everything communicates something, whether you intend it or not.

Because you are always communicating, intentional communication is power.

Another dimension of perception is narrative. Every person carries a story about who they are. Some inherit their narrative from others. Some allow circumstances to write it for them. But the most strategic individuals become authors of their own narrative. They define themselves before someone else attempts to define them. This is not arrogance. It is authorship. When you clearly communicate your identity, values, and direction, you reduce the opportunity for others to misinterpret or mislabel you.

Mislabeling is one of the oldest tools used against rising individuals. If someone cannot control your ability, they may attempt to control how others perceive your ability. They may question your motives. They may frame your confidence as arrogance. They may describe your independence as defiance. These tactics succeed only when you have not already established your own narrative. When your identity is undefined, others can define it for you. When your identity is clear, attempts to distort it appear inconsistent and lose credibility.

Clarity is defense.

Perception also affects opportunity. Many doors open or close based not solely on skill, but on how skill is perceived. Two individuals may possess equal ability, yet the one perceived as prepared, disciplined, and self-directed will often be trusted sooner. Trust accelerates access. Access accelerates advancement. Advancement compounds power. All of this can begin with perception.

This is why those who master perception treat first impressions as strategic moments, not casual ones. They understand that early signals can set long-lasting expectations. They recognize that people tend to remain consistent with their initial judgment. Therefore, they ensure that what others see first aligns with how they wish to be treated.

Controlling perception does not require performance. It requires awareness. It requires understanding what signals you are sending and deciding whether those signals represent you accurately. It requires aligning appearance with intention, tone with message, and behavior with purpose. When these elements match, perception stabilizes. When they conflict, perception fractures.

Consistency strengthens credibility.

The goal is not to manipulate people into believing something false. The goal is to prevent people from forming conclusions about you that are inaccurate or limiting. If you do not shape perception, assumption will shape it for you. Assumptions are rarely neutral. They are built from prior experiences, stereotypes, expectations, and biases. Allowing assumptions to define you is surrendering authorship over your own image.

Those who rise understand a simple truth:

You do not control what everyone thinks of you.

But you can control what you present for them to interpret.

And what you present determines how most people decide to respond.

Principle of Law 4

Perception is the gateway to treatment.

Define yourself first, or be defined by assumption.

Strategic Training Drill, Law 4

Strengthen your perception control with these practices:

Entrance Discipline — Notice how you enter rooms. Adjust posture, pace, and eye focus intentionally.

Tone Awareness — Record yourself speaking. Evaluate clarity, calmness, and authority.

Narrative Statement — Be able to describe who you are and what you stand for in one sentence.

Signal Audit — Ask: "What does my appearance communicate before I speak?"

Consistency Test — Ensure your actions match your stated values.

When perception, intention, and action align, people stop guessing who you are.

They recognize it.

Chapter Five

Law 5 Never Reveal Your Full Strategy Until It Is Already Working

Plans are most powerful when they exist quietly.

Many people lose advantage not because their ideas are weak, but because they expose them too early. They speak before they build. They announce before they establish. They explain before they execute. This habit often comes from excitement, pride, or the desire for validation. Yet in the realm of strategy, premature disclosure weakens position. The moment a plan is revealed, it becomes vulnerable to interference, imitation, criticism, delay, or opposition. What could have developed undisturbed becomes subject to forces you cannot fully control.

Silence protects strategy the way armor protects a warrior.

When others know your full intentions, they can prepare. Preparation changes outcomes. Even those who do not oppose you may unintentionally alter your path simply by reacting to your plans. Advice may confuse your direction. Doubt may slow your momentum. Envy may generate resistance. Curiosity may expose your methods. None of these reactions would occur if your work remained private until it reached a stage of undeniable reality.

There is a difference between a vision and a result. A vision is fragile. A result is undeniable.

Strategic individuals understand that ideas are most delicate during their early stages. At that phase, they require focus, not commentary. They require execution, not explanation. They require refinement, not exposure. When a plan is still forming, outside opinions can distort it. Too many voices dilute clarity. Too much feedback disrupts intuition. Too much visibility invites unnecessary pressure. Protecting your early work allows it to mature without disturbance.

The disciplined strategist reveals outcomes, not intentions.

This does not mean you never share plans. It means you share them selectively and strategically. There are moments when collaboration is necessary, moments when consultation is useful, and moments when visibility strengthens momentum. But those moments are chosen, not impulsive. They occur when disclosure strengthens the plan instead of weakening it. The difference lies in timing.

Timing transforms information into power.

Another reason to guard your strategy is unpredictability. Predictability reduces leverage. If others can foresee your moves, they can adjust before you act. But when your actions arrive without advance warning, they carry greater impact. Surprise compresses reaction time.

Limited reaction time limits resistance. In many situations, the advantage belongs not to the strongest, but to the least predictable.

Unpredictability is not chaos. It is controlled timing.

Revealing your full strategy too early can also shift focus from execution to performance. Once a plan is announced, there is pressure to appear successful rather than to become successful. Energy that should be invested in development becomes invested in presentation. People begin managing perception instead of refining results. The strategy weakens because attention is divided.

Quiet builders avoid this trap. They allow their work to speak only after it has substance.

History repeatedly shows that the most effective movements, innovations, and breakthroughs were not widely visible during their formation. They developed in focused environments, guided by small circles or even by individuals working alone. Only when the foundation was secure did the broader world become aware. By that time, resistance could not stop them because reality had already taken shape.

There is strength in privacy. Privacy concentrates effort. Concentrated effort produces results. Results create influence.

Another dimension of this law concerns protection from opposition. Not everyone who hears your plans wants to see them succeed. Some may doubt you. Some may compete with you. Some may attempt to replicate your idea before you complete it. Some may attempt to discourage you before you begin. Silence prevents unnecessary obstacles from forming prematurely. When people cannot anticipate your direction, they cannot easily obstruct it.

Guarding your strategy is not secrecy for its own sake. It is preservation of momentum.

Strategic restraint also strengthens discipline. When you resist the urge to announce your intentions, you train yourself to prioritize execution over recognition. This builds internal authority. You become less dependent on external approval and more focused on measurable progress. Over time, this habit reshapes your relationship with achievement. You begin to value completion more than attention, substance more than applause.

And when results finally appear, they carry weight precisely because they were not preceded by excessive declaration.

The world often rewards visible success, but it rarely sees the silent preparation behind it. Those who master this law accept that reality. They do not rush exposure. They do not broadcast unfinished work. They do not seek validation for plans still under construction. Instead, they build steadily, quietly, and deliberately until what they have created is strong enough to stand on its own.

When the work is ready, it does not need explanation. It demonstrates itself.

Speak less about what you intend to do.

Show more of what you have done.

Principle of Law 5

Plans spoken too early become targets.

Plans executed quietly become outcomes.

Strategic Training Drill, Law 5

Develop strategic discretion through practice:

Write your next major goal privately instead of announcing it publicly.

Share- plans only with those directly involved in execution.

Delay- public statements until measurable progress exists.

Replace- explanation with demonstration.

Observe- how silence protects focus and accelerates results.

When you learn to guard your intentions, you gain control over timing.

When you control timing, you gain control over impact.

Chapter Six

Law 6 Make Your Presence Felt Without Demanding Attention

There is a form of influence that announces itself loudly, and there is a form of influence that is felt before it is noticed. The first depends on volume. The second depends on presence. Those who do not understand power often try to attract attention in order to be recognized. They raise their voice, exaggerate their movements, dominate conversations, or attempt to command space through force of personality. This approach may create momentary visibility, but it rarely produces lasting authority. Attention gained through noise fades quickly. Presence gained through substance endures.

Presence is not something you demand. It is something you generate.

When a person possesses internal steadiness, clarity of purpose, and disciplined awareness, others sense it without needing explanation. They may not be able to describe what they feel, but they notice it. They listen more closely. They speak more carefully. They adjust their tone. They become more attentive. None of this requires announcement. It occurs because presence communicates before words do.

The mistake many people make is confusing attention with respect. Attention can be obtained instantly. Respect is earned gradually. Attention can be loud. Respect is quiet. Attention seeks reaction. Respect commands consideration. The difference between the two determines whether people merely notice you or whether they take you seriously.

Those who chase attention often reveal insecurity. The need to be seen signals dependence on recognition. Dependence reduces power because it places your sense of value in other people's hands. But those who cultivate presence develop an internal center. They are not trying to be noticed; they are trying to be effective. Ironically, this is what makes them noticeable.

Presence is built through alignment. Your posture aligns with your intention. Your tone aligns with your message. Your actions align with your values. When these elements match, people perceive coherence. Coherence creates trust. Trust creates influence. Influence creates authority. None of this requires performance. It requires consistency.

Consider the individual who enters a room quietly yet shifts the atmosphere simply by arriving. They do not rush. They do not scan anxiously. They do not compete for attention. They observe. They settle. They listen. Within minutes, others begin directing conversation toward them, asking for their input, or adjusting their behavior in response to them. This is not coincidence. It is the effect of contained energy. Energy that is contained feels stronger than energy that is scattered.

Scattered energy looks like urgency. Contained energy looks like control.

Another dimension of presence is restraint. The person who speaks only when necessary creates anticipation. Others begin to listen more carefully because they expect that when this person speaks, it will matter. Words gain value when they are not spent carelessly. Silence, posture, and observation become part of communication. Authority often resides not in what is said, but in how selectively speech is used.

Presence also depends on awareness of environment. Those who carry influence pay attention to the dynamics around them. They notice who is speaking, who is silent, who is leading, who is following, who is tense, who is relaxed. This awareness allows them to move intentionally rather than reactively. They choose when to step forward and when to remain still. They choose when to speak and when to listen. They choose when to engage and when to withdraw. Because their behavior is chosen, it appears deliberate. Deliberate behavior signals confidence.

Confidence that is quiet is often more convincing than confidence that is performed.

Demanding attention can create resistance. People instinctively pull away from those who seem to be forcing recognition. But when presence is felt rather than demanded, resistance decreases. Others become curious instead of defensive. Curiosity opens doors that force cannot. Influence gained through curiosity lasts longer because it is freely given rather than extracted.

To cultivate this kind of presence, you must first become comfortable without constant validation. You must learn to exist in spaces without needing to dominate them. You must trust that substance speaks louder than performance. This requires discipline, because the modern world often rewards display over depth. It encourages constant broadcasting, immediate responses, and visible activity. Yet those who understand power recognize that visibility is not the same as influence. Visibility can be granted. Influence must be built.

The individual with true presence does not chase attention. They attract it unintentionally. Their composure signals stability. Their restraint signals confidence. Their focus signals direction. These signals communicate strength more convincingly than any declaration ever could.

In the long run, people do not remember who spoke the loudest. They remember who moved the room without trying.

Make your presence felt, not forced. When your presence carries weight, your words do not have to.

Principle of Law 6

Attention can be demanded.

Respect must be generated.

Presence is the bridge between the two.

Strategic Training Drill, Law 6

Strengthen your presence through daily practice:

Enter rooms without rushing your movements.

Speak slightly slower than your natural pace.

Maintain eye contact long enough to show steadiness.

Listen fully before responding.

Observe how people adjust when you become calmer instead of louder.

Chapter Seven

Law 7 Guard Your Energy Like a Strategic Resource

Most people manage their time.

Few people manage their energy.

Time is visible. Energy is not. Because energy cannot be seen, it is often spent carelessly. People give it away in arguments that lead nowhere, conversations that drain them, environments that weaken them, and obligations that serve no real purpose. They do not realize that energy is the force behind every action, decision, perception, and result. When energy is scattered, effort becomes weak. When energy is guarded, effort becomes precise. Precision is where power begins.

Every system that influences human behavior understands one fundamental truth: the easiest person to control is the exhausted person. Fatigue weakens judgment. Overstimulation clouds perception. Emotional depletion lowers resistance. When a person is mentally, emotionally, or physically drained, they become more reactive and less deliberate. They respond instead of choosing. They accept instead of evaluating. They comply instead of questioning. Exhaustion reduces discernment, and reduced discernment reduces power.

This is why guarding your energy is not selfish. It is strategic.

Energy is not only physical. It is mental clarity, emotional stability, attention span, and focus. Each of these can be strengthened or depleted depending on how they are used. Every interaction costs energy. Every decision costs energy. Every environment influences energy. Even thoughts consume energy. The disciplined individual recognizes this and begins to treat energy the way a skilled investor treats capital: as something to be allocated wisely, not spent impulsively.

Consider how many situations demand energy without deserving it. Some conversations exist only to provoke reaction. Some debates exist only to waste attention. Some conflicts exist only because someone else lacks discipline. If you respond to every demand placed on your attention, you will spend your energy solving other people's noise instead of building your own direction. Strategic individuals learn to distinguish between what requires response and what merely requests it.

Not every request deserves your energy.

Not every problem is yours to solve.

Not every opinion deserves your attention.

This discernment is a form of strength.

Another reason to guard your energy is that energy determines perception. When you are mentally clear and emotionally steady, you see more accurately. You notice patterns. You detect inconsistencies. You recognize opportunities. But when your energy is depleted, perception narrows. Your thinking becomes shorter, your patience thinner, your reactions faster. The world begins to feel more chaotic, not because chaos increased, but because your capacity to interpret it decreased.

Clarity is impossible without preserved energy.

Those who master themselves understand that attention is one of their most valuable assets. Wherever attention goes, energy follows. Wherever energy flows, results appear. If your attention is constantly pulled toward distractions, irritations, or minor conflicts, your energy will be consumed by them. This leaves little strength for long-term goals, strategic thinking, or meaningful creation. Many people fail not because they lack ability, but because their energy is continually diverted away from what matters most.

Guarding your energy requires boundaries. Boundaries are not barriers against others; they are protections for your focus. They determine what you allow into your mind, your schedule, your environment, and your emotional space. Without boundaries, your energy belongs to whoever demands it most loudly. With boundaries, your energy belongs to your purpose.

The disciplined individual learns to observe where their energy goes each day. They ask themselves: What strengthened me? What drained me? What moved me forward? What pulled me sideways? This awareness transforms energy from something unconscious into something directed. Once energy becomes directed, progress becomes consistent.

There is also a silent authority in those who guard their energy. They do not rush into every conversation. They do not engage every challenge. They do not react to every provocation. Their restraint signals control. Others begin to recognize that their attention is intentional, not automatic. When they choose to focus on something, it carries meaning. When they withdraw attention, it also carries meaning. This selective engagement makes their presence more impactful because it is not given freely.

Energy conserved becomes energy concentrated. Concentrated energy produces momentum. Momentum produces influence. Influence produces results.

Many people try to increase their power by adding more effort. But effort without preserved energy leads to burnout. The wiser approach is to reduce unnecessary expenditure so that the energy you already possess can be directed where it matters. Power is not only about how much you do. It is about how precisely you do it.

The world will always present reasons to spend your energy. Some are necessary. Many are not. The difference between those who advance and those who remain stuck is often the ability to distinguish between the two. The disciplined mind does not give energy simply because something demands it. It gives energy because it chooses to.

Guarding your energy is not withdrawal from life. It is preparation for meaningful action. When your energy is preserved, your decisions improve. When your decisions improve, your outcomes strengthen. And when your outcomes strengthen, your influence grows.

Those who waste energy chase results.

Those who guard energy create them.

Principle of Law 7

Energy is the fuel of power.

Whoever controls where their energy goes controls where their life goes.

Strategic Training Drill, Law 7

Build energy discipline with these practices:

Notice which conversations leave you strengthened and which leave you drained.

Limit engagement with situations that consistently reduce your clarity.

Schedule focused work periods free from interruption.

Pause before responding to emotional stimuli.

Ask daily: Did I spend energy or invest it?

Over time you will discover a quiet transformation:

The less energy you waste, the more power you possess.

Chapter Eight

Law 8 Control Your Emotional Signals Before Others Use Them

Emotion is natural.

Uncontrolled emotion is readable.

Readable emotion is usable.

Most people believe their emotions belong only to them. In reality, emotions are constantly broadcasting signals to everyone around them. Facial expressions shift. Tone changes. Posture tightens. Breathing alters. Timing speeds up or slows down. Even silence can communicate agitation, confidence, fear, impatience, or certainty. Human beings are highly perceptive to these signals, often without realizing it. We instinctively read one another. We sense tension. We sense hesitation. We sense insecurity. We sense excitement. And once someone can read your emotional state, they can adjust their behavior accordingly.

This is why emotional discipline is not suppression. It is strategic control.

The person who cannot regulate their emotional signals becomes predictable. Predictability gives others information. Information gives others leverage. If someone knows what frustrates you, they can provoke you. If they know what flatters you, they can influence you. If they know what intimidates you, they can pressure you. If they know what excites you, they can distract you. In each case, your reaction becomes their tool.

The disciplined individual understands that feelings are internal experiences, not automatic instructions. Feeling anger does not require acting angry. Feeling fear does not require appearing afraid. Feeling excitement does not require revealing anticipation. Between feeling and expression lies choice. That space is where power lives.

Many environments, professional, social, competitive, or institutional, test emotional control constantly. A comment may challenge your authority. A situation may feel unfair. A conversation may carry hidden tension. A decision may not go your way. These moments are not only events; they are assessments. They reveal whether you are governed by impulse or by intention. Those who react instantly often believe they are showing strength, when in fact they are showing exposure. Reaction reveals the location of your emotional triggers. Once your triggers are known, they can be pressed again.

Calmness conceals leverage. Reaction exposes it.

This is why composed individuals are often perceived as powerful even when they say very little. Their steadiness creates uncertainty for others. If someone cannot read your emotional state, they cannot easily predict your response. If they cannot predict your response, they cannot easily manipulate the interaction. Emotional composure introduces ambiguity, and ambiguity protects position.

Another reason to control emotional signals is that perception shapes reality. People often respond less to what is happening and more to how someone appears to interpret what is happening. If you remain composed in pressure, others assume you understand something they do not. If you stay calm in conflict, others assume you are confident in your position. If you maintain balance in uncertainty, others assume you possess stability. Whether or not they consciously analyze it, they feel it. And feeling influences behavior.

Emotional discipline also protects your decision-making. Strong emotional reactions narrow focus. They push attention toward the immediate moment and away from long-term consequences. In that state, choices become shorter, sharper, and often less accurate. But when emotion is steady, perception widens. You see more variables. You consider more outcomes. You recognize patterns others miss. A calm mind does not eliminate emotion; it directs it. Directed emotion strengthens judgment instead of distorting it.

There is a difference between feeling and displaying. Mature strength understands that emotions are information, not commands. Anger can signal injustice. Fear can signal risk. Excitement can signal opportunity. But signals are meant to be interpreted, not obeyed automatically. The strategic individual listens to emotion internally while presenting composure externally. This creates two advantages: insight within, stability without.

This balance cannot be faked for long. It must be trained. Emotional discipline develops through awareness. You begin by noticing your own reactions as they arise. You observe what situations tighten your chest, quicken your speech, or change your tone. You identify patterns. Once you can see your patterns, you can manage them. Awareness precedes control.

Control precedes power.

Another overlooked truth is that visible emotional volatility often reduces credibility. People may tolerate it briefly, but they rarely trust it. Stability attracts responsibility. Instability repels it. When others see that your emotional state remains steady across different circumstances, they begin to rely on you. Reliability builds influence. Influence builds authority.

This does not mean becoming expressionless or detached from humanity. It means becoming deliberate. You choose when to show emotion and when to reserve it. You choose when passion strengthens your message and when calmness strengthens your position. Choice is the defining line between discipline and impulse.

Those who cannot control their signals communicate more than they intend.

Those who master their signals communicate only what they choose.

In environments shaped by competition, negotiation, or evaluation, this difference determines outcomes. Emotional composure is not merely a personality trait. It is a strategic asset. It protects your leverage, strengthens your perception, and sharpens your decisions simultaneously.

When your emotions are under your command, your presence becomes steady.

When your presence is steady, your influence becomes durable.

Principle of Law 8

Emotion is power when directed.

Emotion is vulnerability when uncontrolled.

Master the signal, and you master the exchange.

Strategic Training Drill, Law 8

Strengthen emotional command through these practices:

When triggered, pause and identify the feeling before responding.

Slow your breathing during tense moments.

Lower your voice instead of raising it.

Maintain neutral posture when challenged.

Ask yourself: Am I choosing this reaction, or is it choosing me?

With practice, something remarkable happens:

You stop being steered by emotion and start steering with it.

Chapter Nine

PART II The Architecture of Influence How to Build Position, Authority, and Irreplaceable Value

PART II Law 9 Study the System Before You Try to Move Within It

The Architecture of Influence

How to Build Position, Authority, and Irreplaceable Value

Power begins internally. But influence is built externally.

The first phase of this book focused on self-command, mastering perception, discipline, positioning, silence, energy, and awareness. These are the inner mechanics of power. Without them, any attempt to influence the outside world collapses under pressure. Internal command creates stability. Stability creates presence. Presence creates credibility. Credibility creates access.

Now the path advances.

Part II shifts from personal mastery to strategic impact. Here you will learn how influence is constructed, how authority is recognized, how credibility is multiplied, and how positioning becomes leverage. These laws do not merely teach you how to improve yourself; they teach you how to shape environments, guide outcomes, and move within systems with intention rather than chance.

Most people spend their lives reacting to circumstances. A smaller number learn how to navigate circumstances. But the rare individual learns how to shape circumstances. That is the purpose of this phase. You will begin to understand how influence is built layer by layer, how reputations form, how trust compounds, how credibility expands, and how power becomes visible without needing to be announced.

Influence is not noise. It is structure.

It is not granted randomly. It is constructed deliberately.

And like any structure, it follows principles. These principles govern how people respond, how systems behave, how opportunities form, and how momentum develops. Once you understand these principles, you stop relying on chance and start relying on design. You begin to recognize patterns others overlook. You see openings others miss. You anticipate shifts before they occur. You move with timing instead of urgency.

This section is about building the architecture that allows your presence to carry weight wherever you go.

Because the goal is not simply to possess ability.

The goal is to become positioned so that ability is recognized, trusted, and sought.

Those who master this phase stop trying to prove themselves.

They become undeniable.

Part II Principle

Inner power earns self-respect.

Structured influence earns world respect.

Law 9

Every environment has a structure.

Every structure has rules.

Every rule has a pattern.

And every pattern reveals leverage.

Many people attempt to succeed within systems they do not understand. They enter institutions, industries, organizations, and social hierarchies assuming that effort alone determines outcome. Effort is important, but effort without structural awareness often leads to frustration. When someone works hard yet fails to advance, they may believe they lack ability. In reality, they may simply lack understanding of the system they are operating within. Without that understanding, they move blindly. Blind movement wastes energy. Informed movement multiplies it.

A system is not just an organization or institution. A system is any environment governed by patterns, spoken or unspoken. Workplaces are systems. Social circles are systems. Markets are systems. Governments are systems. Even conversations are systems. Each contains rules that determine how influence flows, how decisions are made, and how opportunities appear. Some rules are written. Many are not. The unwritten ones are often the most important, because they determine behavior without announcing themselves.

Those who rise quickly in any field share one habit: before they try to change the system, they study it.

They observe how authority actually operates, not how it is described. They watch who speaks and who is listened to. They notice which actions are rewarded and which are ignored. They track how decisions really get made, not how official policies claim they are made. They identify which signals lead to advancement and which lead to resistance. In doing so, they begin to see the system as it functions, rather than as it is advertised.

There is often a difference between the stated structure and the real structure. The stated structure is what people say exists. The real structure is what actually determines outcomes. Power belongs to those who learn to distinguish between the two.

Understanding systems provides several advantages at once. First, it prevents wasted effort. When you know how something operates, you can align your actions with its mechanics instead of working against them unknowingly. Second, it reveals leverage points. Every system has places where small actions create large effects. These points are rarely obvious to those who have not studied the structure. Third, it protects you from manipulation. When you understand how a system works, you can recognize when someone is trying to use it against you.

Ignorance of structure creates vulnerability. Awareness of structure creates choice.

Many people attempt to challenge systems before they understand them. They react to what they see on the surface without examining what lies beneath. This often leads to misdirected effort. They push in areas where resistance is strongest and ignore areas where change would be easier. They confront symptoms instead of causes. They expend energy without producing results. The disciplined strategist does the opposite. They study quietly first. They map relationships, incentives, and outcomes. They observe patterns long enough to see where movement is possible.

Study precedes strategy. Strategy precedes action.

Systems also operate on incentives. Incentives determine behavior more reliably than rules. If you want to understand why something happens repeatedly, ask what is being rewarded. Rewards may be money, status, approval, recognition, security, or access. Whatever is rewarded becomes repeated. Whatever is ignored becomes rare. Once you understand incentives, you understand direction. And once you understand direction, you can anticipate movement.

Another important element of systems is timing. Systems do not remain static. They shift, evolve, and adapt. Conditions change. Leadership changes. Priorities change. Public opinion changes. A system that is rigid today may become flexible tomorrow. A system that appears open today may close later. Those who study systems continuously learn to recognize these shifts. They sense when pressure is building, when opportunities are forming, and when resistance is weakening. This awareness allows them to act at moments when their effort will have the greatest effect.

Timing without understanding is luck.

Timing with understanding is strategy.

Studying systems also strengthens patience. When you see how structures operate, you realize that outcomes often depend on positioning rather than speed. Instead of rushing, you begin placing yourself where opportunity is most likely to appear. Positioning reduces struggle. It allows progress to occur with less resistance because you are moving with the structure instead of against it.

This law is not about conformity. It is about comprehension. Understanding a system does not mean you must agree with it. It means you understand it well enough to navigate it intelligently. Once you understand a structure, you gain options. You can move within it, around it, or beyond it. But you cannot move effectively until you know what you are dealing with.

Those who ignore systems are shaped by them.

Those who study systems learn how to shape outcomes within them.

The most effective individuals are rarely the loudest or the fastest. They are the most observant. They treat every environment as something to be read before it is acted upon. They gather information before they invest effort. They learn patterns before they attempt influence. They understand that clarity about structure turns confusion into strategy.

If you want to move with precision, begin with observation. If you want to act with power, begin with understanding. Because once you see how a system truly works, you stop guessing where to step.

You start choosing.

Principle of Law 9

Do not fight what you have not studied.

Do not enter what you have not mapped.

Understanding the system is the first move inside it.

Strategic Training Drill, Law 9

Develop structural awareness daily:

Observe who holds real influence in any room you enter.

Identify what behaviors are rewarded in your environment.

Watch patterns instead of isolated events.

Ask what incentives drive decisions around you.

Study quietly before acting publicly.

As this habit develops, you will notice something others miss:

Most people move inside systems.

Few people understand them.

Those who understand them decide how they move.

Chapter Ten

Law 10 Position Yourself Where Opportunity Must Pass You

Most people chase opportunity.

The disciplined strategist positions themselves so opportunity must come to them.

This distinction separates effort from leverage.

Chasing opportunity is exhausting. It requires constant movement, constant searching, constant reacting. It places you in pursuit mode, where you must continually prove, persuade, and compete for attention. Positioning, on the other hand, shifts the dynamic. Instead of running toward possibility, you place yourself where possibility naturally flows. When positioned correctly, you no longer have to chase every opening. The right openings begin to find you.

This is not luck. It is design.

Every environment contains channels through which opportunity travels. Information flows through certain people. Resources move through certain networks. Decisions pass through certain rooms. Visibility concentrates in certain spaces. Influence circulates among certain groups. Those who do not study these pathways wander randomly, hoping to encounter chance. Those who understand them place themselves deliberately along those routes.

Position determines access. Access determines options. Options determine outcomes.

Many people fail not because they lack talent, but because they remain in positions where their talent cannot be seen, used, or rewarded. Ability hidden in the wrong environment produces little effect. The same ability placed in the right environment multiplies rapidly. This is why changing position can sometimes produce more progress than increasing effort. Effort improves performance. Position determines whether performance is noticed.

Consider how water behaves. Water does not struggle to flow uphill. It follows gravity. Opportunity behaves similarly. It follows structure, incentives, and visibility. If you place yourself where these forces naturally move, progress becomes easier. If you remain outside those pathways, progress becomes harder no matter how capable you are.

Strategic individuals therefore ask a different question than most people. Instead of asking, "How do I find opportunity?" they ask, "Where does opportunity already flow?" This shift in thinking transforms how they act. They begin studying environments instead of chasing outcomes. They observe where decisions are made. They identify where information originates. They locate where influence concentrates. Once they see these points, they move closer to them.

Proximity increases probability.

Being near opportunity changes what you see and what you are offered. It exposes you to conversations others never hear. It allows you to notice openings before they become obvious. It introduces you to individuals who shape direction. It places you in positions where your presence is remembered. Often, advancement is not about convincing the entire world of your value. It is about being present where the right people can see it.

Positioning also affects perception. When you are consistently seen in environments associated with competence, discipline, or leadership, others begin associating you with those qualities. This association forms quietly, without announcement. Over time, people begin to assume you belong in those spaces. Once that assumption forms, doors open more easily because your presence feels natural rather than surprising.

This is why the disciplined strategist chooses environments carefully. They do not remain in places that conceal their ability or restrict their growth. They seek environments where their effort produces visible results. They understand that environment is not merely background; it is multiplier. The right environment amplifies your strengths. The wrong environment drains them.

Strategic Clarification Do Not Confuse Demand With Opportunity

At first encounter, some readers assume this law means placing yourself wherever the most work is needed. This interpretation sounds reasonable, but it is incomplete and potentially dangerous. Demand for labor and flow of opportunity are not the same thing. Understanding the difference is essential, because confusing them can place a person in environments that consume effort while offering little advancement.

An environment can require enormous work yet provide very little opportunity. Some places need the most effort precisely because they lack direction, structure, or growth. They may demand constant output but offer no pathway upward. They may rely on labor yet rarely reward initiative. In such environments, a person can work tirelessly and still remain in the same position. Effort alone cannot compensate for poor placement.

Opportunity does not usually flow where effort is highest.

Opportunity flows where momentum exists.

Momentum appears where decisions are being made, where resources are moving, where expansion is occurring, and where influence is concentrated. These environments generate openings because activity produces access. Access creates visibility. Visibility creates recognition. Recognition creates advancement. When you place yourself near these channels, progress becomes possible not only because of what you do, but because of where you are.

Instead of asking, "Where am I needed most?" the disciplined thinker asks, "Where is growth already happening?" This question shifts focus from obligation to leverage. Being needed can make you busy. Being positioned can make you effective. Busyness consumes energy. Effectiveness multiplies it.

The difference is not effort.

The difference is placement.

Strategic individuals study environments before committing themselves to them. They observe whether growth is occurring or merely promised. They look for movement rather than noise. They notice where advancement has already happened for others. They pay attention to where decisions originate instead of where instructions are delivered. These observations reveal whether an environment is a channel of opportunity or simply a container of labor.

The highest form of positioning is not simply being where opportunity exists. It is being where opportunity must pass through. When your role, location, or skill places you at a junction point, where information, decisions, or resources move, you gain a form of influence that effort alone cannot create. At that level, opportunities begin to approach you instead of the other way around. People seek your involvement. Doors open in your direction. Choices increase. Freedom expands.

This is the true aim of Law 10: not endless work, but strategic placement.

Positioning also includes timing. Being in the right place at the wrong time can be as ineffective as being in the wrong place entirely. Strategic positioning therefore includes awareness of momentum. When a field is expanding, positioning yourself within it early can create advantages that last for years. When a system is shifting, placing yourself near its emerging center can produce opportunities others do not yet see. Timing and position together create leverage that effort alone cannot replicate.

There is also a quiet authority that comes from consistent positioning. When people repeatedly see you in spaces of purpose, they begin to associate you with purpose. Familiarity builds recognition. Recognition builds trust. Trust builds influence. Influence creates opportunity. What appears to be sudden success is often the result of sustained positioning.

Those who understand this law do not rely solely on effort to advance. They rely on placement. They place themselves where conversations of consequence occur. They place themselves where decisions are shaped. They place themselves where growth is visible. They place themselves where momentum is building. In doing so, they reduce the distance between themselves and opportunity.

You cannot control every opportunity that exists.

But you can control how close you stand to where it travels.

Position is silent power. It does not announce itself, yet it determines access. It does not demand attention, yet it shapes outcome. It does not replace effort, yet it multiplies it. When your position is strategic, your actions produce greater effect with less strain.

The person who understands positioning stops wandering. They begin placing.

And once they are placed correctly, opportunity no longer has to be chased.

It arrives.

Principle of Law 10

Do not spend your life chasing doors.

Stand where doors are opened.

Precision Principle

Do not place yourself where labor is constant.

Place yourself where outcomes are decided.

Strategic Training Drill, Law 10

Identify where decisions are made in your environment.

Spend more time in spaces where growth is happening.

Move closer to people who create opportunity, not just talk about it.

Evaluate whether your environment multiplies or limits your ability.

Ask daily: Am I chasing opportunity, or am I positioned for it?

Over time you will notice a transformation:

The harder you work on your position, the less you must chase results.

Chapter Eleven

Law 11 Become Valuable Enough That You Cannot Be Ignored

Power that must be demanded is fragile.

Power that is sought is durable.

Many people spend years attempting to convince others to recognize their importance. They speak about their abilities, emphasize their effort, and remind people of what they believe they deserve. Yet recognition obtained through insistence rarely produces lasting authority. True influence develops differently. It grows when a person becomes consistently valuable in ways that others depend on.

Value is the true foundation of influence.

When someone repeatedly contributes in ways that improve outcomes, solve problems, or strengthen results, their presence begins to carry weight. People begin to notice the difference when they are involved and when they are not. Conversations begin to include them naturally. Decisions begin to consider their perspective. Opportunities begin to involve them. Not because they demanded recognition, but because excluding them would reduce the quality of the outcome.

This is when influence stops being requested and starts being expected.

Many people misunderstand what creates value. They assume it is talent alone. Talent is only the starting point. Value is created when ability becomes useful. A skill becomes powerful when it consistently solves problems that matter to others. When someone demonstrates this usefulness repeatedly, their reliability becomes visible. Reliability builds trust. Trust builds dependence. And dependence is one of the quiet foundations of influence.

Reliability often matters more than brilliance.

A single impressive performance can attract attention, but consistent effectiveness builds reputation. Reputation is memory attached to perception. When people repeatedly observe that your involvement improves results, they begin to associate your presence with competence. That association becomes a silent advocate for you, even in spaces where you are not present.

Over time, this memory becomes influence.

There is another dimension of value that strengthens this process: distinctiveness. If what you contribute can easily be replaced, your influence will remain limited. But when your combination of skill, perspective, judgment, and discipline becomes difficult to duplicate, your presence gains strategic weight. Distinctiveness does not require extraordinary talent. It requires consistent usefulness in a way others cannot easily replicate.

Irreplaceability is not claimed.

It is demonstrated.

Those who understand this law do not focus primarily on appearing important. Instead, they focus on becoming useful in ways that environments genuinely need. They observe which abilities produce results. They notice where others struggle to deliver consistency. Then they cultivate mastery in those areas. Over time, this focus transforms their position. Instead of competing for recognition, they become someone recognition gravitates toward.

When value becomes visible, authority begins to form naturally.

Another advantage of becoming indispensable is resilience. Environments change constantly. Leadership shifts. Institutions reorganize. Conditions evolve. In uncertain environments, individuals who consistently deliver meaningful results remain valuable regardless of circumstance. Their usefulness allows them to move across changing structures because their contribution is recognized beyond any single role.

This kind of value functions as stability within instability.

Building this level of influence requires patience. Value accumulates over time through repeated demonstration. Each project, decision, and action contributes to a reputation that gradually becomes difficult to overlook. Those who think long-term choose substance over spectacle. They prioritize reliability over attention. They invest in effectiveness rather than performance.

Because lasting authority grows slowly, but it grows deeply.

There is also humility in genuine value. Individuals who possess it rarely need to announce themselves. Their work speaks before they do. Their results introduce them before their words ever attempt to.

Others recognize their importance not because it was declared, but because it was observed.

Quiet competence often carries more authority than loud self-promotion.

The ultimate goal is not admiration. Admiration fades quickly. The goal is usefulness that improves outcomes. When people know that your involvement strengthens results, they begin to seek it. When your absence weakens outcomes, they begin to notice it. When both conditions are true, your value has reached a level that cannot easily be ignored.

At that point, influence no longer needs to be pursued.

It arrives.

Principle of Law 11

Do not pursue recognition.

Pursue usefulness so undeniable that recognition pursues you.

Strategic Training Drill, Law 11

Strengthen your strategic value.

Identify one skill that consistently solves meaningful problems.

Develop that skill until your results become noticeable.

Deliver reliability instead of occasional brilliance.

Study where others struggle and master that space.

Ask yourself regularly:

If I were absent, what would become harder without me?

When the answer becomes clear to others, your value has begun to take shape.

And once your value becomes undeniable, influence follows naturally.

Chapter Twelve

Chapter 12 Control Access to Yourself to Increase Your Value

Value increases when access decreases.

Many people believe that influence grows by making themselves constantly available. They respond to every message, attend every request, participate in every conversation, and attempt to be present in every situation where they might be needed. While this may create temporary visibility, it often reduces perceived value. When someone is always available, their presence begins to feel ordinary. When something feels ordinary, it loses significance.

Scarcity is one of the oldest principles of value.

In economics, objects become valuable when they are limited. The same principle applies to attention, time, and presence. When access to someone is unrestricted, their contribution can be taken for granted. But when access becomes intentional and selective, their time begins to carry weight. People recognize that engaging with them requires purpose. This recognition transforms ordinary interaction into meaningful engagement.

Scarcity does not mean isolation.

It means intentional availability.

The disciplined strategist understands that time and attention are finite resources. Every conversation, meeting, request, or obligation consumes energy. When these resources are spent without intention, the result is exhaustion and diluted effectiveness. But when access is carefully managed, energy remains concentrated. Concentrated energy improves clarity, judgment, and impact.

This concentration changes how others perceive you.

People instinctively notice patterns of availability. When someone responds immediately to every request, others assume that their time carries little cost. When someone responds thoughtfully and selectively, others assume their time carries greater value. This perception alters behavior. Requests become more purposeful. Conversations become more focused. Interactions become more respectful.

Scarcity creates seriousness.

There is also a psychological effect at work. Humans tend to appreciate what requires effort to obtain. When access requires patience or preparation, people approach the interaction more thoughtfully. They listen more carefully. They prepare more thoroughly. They value the exchange more deeply. In contrast, unlimited access often leads to casual treatment because nothing feels at stake.

This is why many influential individuals maintain structured boundaries around their time. They do not respond instantly to every request. They limit how frequently they engage. They protect periods of uninterrupted focus. These boundaries are not barriers against others; they are protections for effectiveness. They ensure that when attention is given, it is meaningful rather than scattered.

Boundaries protect value.

Another important function of controlled access is protection from distraction. The modern environment constantly competes for attention. Messages arrive continuously. Notifications demand immediate response. Conversations begin without purpose. If every demand receives attention, focus becomes fragmented. Fragmented focus weakens productivity and reduces the quality of decisions. But when access is regulated, attention can remain directed toward work that truly matters.

Directed attention produces stronger outcomes.

Controlling access also encourages independence among those around you. When individuals know they cannot rely on immediate availability, they often develop stronger problem-solving abilities themselves. They prepare more carefully before approaching you. They think through situations more thoroughly. In this way, boundaries not only protect your energy, they strengthen the capabilities of those around you.

This creates a healthier environment of responsibility and respect.

However, controlling access requires balance. If taken too far, it can create distance that appears arrogant or dismissive. Influence thrives on trust, and trust requires approachability. The key is intentional openness. When you choose to engage, do so with full attention. When you speak, be present. When you contribute, make it meaningful. In this way, limited access increases the quality of each interaction rather than reducing it.

Quality replaces quantity.

Over time, this pattern reshapes how others perceive you. Your time becomes associated with purpose. Your attention becomes associated with focus. Your presence becomes associated with importance. People begin to prepare before engaging with you because they know the interaction matters. This subtle shift elevates your position without requiring any declaration of authority.

Authority emerges through pattern, not proclamation.

Those who master this law do not disappear from the world. Instead, they become deliberate in how they appear within it. They choose moments carefully. They speak when their contribution improves the situation. They participate when their involvement strengthens the outcome. And when they withdraw, they do so without explanation because their boundaries are already understood.

This discipline protects both value and energy.

In environments where attention is constantly demanded, the individual who controls access to themselves possesses a quiet advantage. Their time remains focused. Their attention remains strong. Their presence remains meaningful. Over time, these qualities increase their influence naturally.

Because what is always available becomes ordinary.

What is carefully given becomes valuable.

Principle of Law 12

Unlimited access reduces value.

Intentional access increases influence.

Strategic Training Drill, Law 12

Develop intentional access:

Protect specific periods for uninterrupted work.

Respond thoughtfully instead of immediately when possible.

Accept fewer commitments, but fulfill them with full attention.

Notice which requests genuinely require your involvement.

Ask yourself regularly:

Am I giving my attention intentionally, or automatically?

As you practice this discipline, something important happens:

People begin to respect your time because you respect it first.

Chapter Thirteen

Chapter 13 Shape Your Reputation Before Others Shape It

Your reputation enters the room before you do.

Every environment forms impressions about people long before they speak. Conversations occur privately. Observations accumulate quietly. Experiences are remembered and repeated. From these fragments, a narrative begins to form about who someone is, what they represent, and how they should be treated.

This narrative becomes reputation.

Reputation functions as a shortcut for judgment. Because individuals rarely have time to analyze every person deeply, they rely on remembered patterns. If someone has consistently demonstrated competence, they are approached with confidence. If someone has shown unreliability, they are approached with caution. If someone has displayed discipline, they are trusted with responsibility. These conclusions form long before formal evaluation ever occurs.

Reputation becomes a form of social memory.

Many people make the mistake of ignoring reputation until it has already been defined by others. They assume that their work alone will eventually correct misunderstandings. Unfortunately, once a narrative becomes established, it becomes difficult to change. Perceptions tend to reinforce themselves. People interpret new actions through the lens of existing beliefs. If someone is perceived as careless, even their careful actions may be doubted. If someone is perceived as dependable, even small mistakes may be forgiven.

Because perception shapes interpretation.

For this reason, strategic individuals actively shape how they are known. They understand that reputation grows from patterns, not from occasional gestures. Every action contributes to a larger picture. The way someone speaks, responds, solves problems, handles pressure, and treats others gradually forms a consistent image in the minds of observers.

Consistency builds reputation.

One of the most powerful elements of reputation is reliability. When people know what to expect from someone, they begin to trust that expectation. If someone repeatedly demonstrates calm judgment during conflict, they become known as a stabilizing presence. If someone consistently delivers high-quality work, they become known for excellence. Over time, these patterns accumulate into a reputation that begins to speak for them.

And once reputation begins to speak, it becomes an advocate.

Another important aspect of reputation is integrity. Integrity means alignment between words and actions. When promises are kept and standards are maintained even under pressure, observers notice. Integrity produces credibility because it demonstrates that someone's behavior does not change when circumstances become difficult.

Credibility strengthens reputation.

However, reputation can also be damaged quickly when behavior contradicts previously established patterns. A moment of dishonesty, disrespect, or carelessness can spread rapidly through social networks. Because negative information tends to travel faster than positive information, protecting reputation requires constant awareness. Strategic individuals recognize that their conduct in both visible and private settings contributes to how they are perceived.

Reputation is always being recorded.

There is also an element of narrative control involved in shaping reputation. If someone never defines themselves, others will do it for them. People fill gaps in understanding with assumptions. These assumptions often reflect stereotypes, misunderstandings, or incomplete information. To prevent this, strategic individuals communicate their principles clearly through their actions, choices, and standards.

They allow their behavior to explain who they are.

Importantly, shaping reputation does not require self-promotion. Loud declarations of excellence rarely convince observers. Instead, reputation is built through repeated demonstration. When someone consistently behaves with discipline, competence, fairness, and responsibility, observers eventually recognize these traits without needing them to be announced.

Actions establish reputation more effectively than claims.

Over time, a strong reputation begins to function as protection. When challenges arise or accusations appear, a history of consistent behavior creates credibility. People who know the individual may question the accusation rather than immediately believing it. This protective effect is one of the greatest advantages of a well-established reputation.

Reputation becomes a shield.

It also becomes an opportunity generator. Individuals with positive reputations are more likely to be recommended for leadership roles, trusted with responsibility, and invited into meaningful collaborations. Others seek their involvement because their past performance suggests future reliability.

Opportunity follows reputation.

Those who understand this law treat reputation as a strategic asset. They think carefully about how each action contributes to the larger narrative others will remember. They recognize that influence does not come from a single moment of success, but from the accumulation of trustworthy behavior over time.

Reputation is not built in one day.

But it can be damaged in one moment.

For this reason, disciplined individuals continually evaluate how their conduct reflects their values. They avoid actions that contradict the character they wish to establish. They maintain consistency even when circumstances encourage shortcuts. By doing so, they gradually construct a reputation that reflects their true principles.

And when reputation aligns with character, influence becomes sustainable.

Because people may question what you say.

They may even question what you do.

But when your reputation consistently confirms your character, your presence begins to carry authority.

Principle of Law 13

Reputation is the identity that travels ahead of you.

Shape it intentionally before others define it for you.

Strategic Training Drill, Law 13

Strengthen your reputation intentionally.

Identify three qualities you want to be known for (discipline, reliability, fairness, etc.).

Demonstrate those qualities consistently in daily actions.

Avoid behaviors that contradict the reputation you wish to build.

Deliver on commitments even when it is inconvenient.

Ask yourself regularly:

If someone described me when I am not present, what would they say?

Your reputation is the story others tell about you when you are absent.

Make sure it reflects the truth you want remembered.

Chapter Fourteen

Chapter 14 Use Patience as Strategic Power

The impatient mind is easily controlled.

Most systems, institutions, and conflicts are designed around a simple human weakness: the desire for immediate results. People want recognition quickly. They want advancement quickly. They want justice quickly. Because of this impatience, individuals often reveal their plans too early, act before conditions are ready, or exhaust their energy in short bursts of effort.

Those who understand strategy recognize that time itself can be used as a weapon.

Patience is not passive waiting.

It is controlled timing.

A patient strategist observes carefully before acting. Instead of rushing to respond to every provocation, they analyze the environment, the personalities involved, and the possible consequences of each move. While others react emotionally or impulsively, the patient individual gathers information and prepares their response deliberately.

This delay creates clarity.

Many conflicts are lost because individuals respond immediately to pressure. When provoked, they react emotionally rather than strategically. Their reactions expose weaknesses, intentions, or vulnerabilities. Once these elements become visible, opponents can predict their behavior.

Impatience reveals strategy before it is ready.

Patience, on the other hand, allows a person to remain unpredictable. When someone refuses to react immediately, observers cannot easily determine their intentions. This uncertainty forces others to hesitate. Hesitation creates space. And space allows the patient strategist to decide when and how to act.

Time becomes an ally.

Patience also allows patterns to reveal themselves. Human behavior tends to repeat. People expose their motivations through repeated actions, language, and decisions. Someone who waits long enough begins to see these patterns clearly. When patterns become visible, the strategist gains insight into how situations will likely develop.

Insight produces advantage.

Another benefit of patience is endurance. Many conflicts are not decided by a single dramatic moment but by sustained effort over long periods. Individuals who rely only on bursts of enthusiasm often lose momentum when progress appears slow. In contrast, those who cultivate patience maintain steady focus. They continue building, learning, and adjusting even when recognition is delayed.

Endurance outlasts excitement.

Patience also protects emotional discipline. When individuals feel rushed or pressured, they may compromise their standards or accept unfavorable outcomes simply to resolve discomfort. Strategic patience prevents this. It allows someone to wait until conditions align with their objectives rather than settling for immediate but limited results.

Timing becomes intentional rather than reactive.

This law also teaches restraint. Not every opportunity requires immediate action. Some opportunities improve with time as more information becomes available or circumstances evolve. The patient individual learns to recognize the difference between moments that require quick response and moments that reward careful preparation.

Wisdom lies in knowing the difference.

Importantly, patience does not mean inactivity. While others may appear idle, they are often working quietly beneath the surface, studying systems, strengthening skills, building relationships, and refining plans. By the time they act publicly, the groundwork for success has already been laid.

Preparation makes timing effective.

Those who master patience understand that the world often rewards persistence more than urgency. Many significant achievements require sustained effort across years rather than weeks. Impatient individuals abandon their plans too early because results do not appear immediately. Patient individuals continue refining their approach until progress becomes unavoidable.

Time amplifies disciplined effort.

There is also psychological power in patience. When someone remains calm while others become agitated, they gain a subtle advantage in negotiations, conflicts, and decision-making. Calmness signals control. Control influences perception. People often trust the individual who appears composed under pressure.

Composure creates authority.

Over time, this disciplined patience transforms how others respond to you. People recognize that you do not react impulsively. They realize that your actions are deliberate rather than emotional. This recognition encourages respect, because deliberate action suggests thoughtful judgment.

And thoughtful judgment inspires confidence.

Ultimately, patience allows a person to align action with the right moment. Strategy is not simply about knowing what to do. It is about knowing when to do it. Acting too early can destroy an opportunity. Acting too late can allow it to disappear. But acting at the right time can multiply the effectiveness of even a small effort.

Timing is power.

Those who cultivate patience develop the ability to observe, prepare, and strike with precision rather than urgency. They conserve energy for the moments that truly matter. They remain calm when others rush. They wait when others panic. And when the time arrives, their actions carry greater impact because they are supported by preparation and clarity.

Because the person who controls their timing often controls the outcome.

Principle of Law 14

Patience transforms time into a strategic advantage.

Do not rush into action simply because others demand it.

Act when conditions serve your purpose.

Strategic Training Drill, Law 14

Strengthen strategic patience:

Delay emotional reactions when confronted with pressure.

Observe patterns before making major decisions.

Prepare quietly while others rush publicly.

Identify the difference between urgency and importance.

Ask yourself regularly:

Am I reacting to pressure, or choosing the right moment to act?

Patience does not slow success.

It aligns success with the right moment.

Chapter Fifteen

Chapter 15 Speak With Precision, Not Excess

Words create realities.

Every conversation shapes perception. Every statement contributes to how others understand your intentions, your intelligence, and your character. Yet many people weaken their influence through excessive speaking. They explain too much, defend themselves unnecessarily, or fill silence simply to avoid discomfort.

In doing so, they dilute the power of their own words.

The disciplined communicator understands that influence does not come from the number of words spoken. It comes from the clarity and purpose of those words. When someone speaks carefully and deliberately, each statement carries greater weight. Listeners pay closer attention because the speaker does not waste language.

Precision creates authority.

Silence plays an important role in this process. Silence allows thoughts to form fully before being expressed. It prevents emotional reactions from turning into careless statements. It also encourages others to reveal more about themselves, because people often continue speaking when confronted with thoughtful quietness.

Strategic silence gathers information.

Many conflicts escalate because individuals respond impulsively to statements that provoke emotion. Anger, frustration, or pride can cause someone to speak quickly in defense of themselves. These reactions often produce words that later require explanation or apology. By practicing restraint, a person avoids exposing unnecessary vulnerabilities.

Controlled speech protects reputation.

Precision also improves understanding. When language is clear and direct, misunderstandings decrease. People know exactly what was meant because the statement leaves little room for confusion. In contrast, vague or excessive explanations can obscure the main point and allow others to interpret meaning differently.

Clarity strengthens communication.

Another advantage of disciplined language is respect. Individuals who choose their words carefully demonstrate that they value thoughtful expression. This habit signals maturity and self-control. Over time, listeners begin to trust that when this person speaks, their words have been considered carefully rather than produced impulsively.

Trust grows from reliability.

Precision also increases persuasion. When arguments are concise and structured, listeners can follow the logic easily. They focus on the idea rather than being distracted by unnecessary details. Persuasive speakers understand that strong ideas often require fewer words, not more.

Economy strengthens impact.

This law does not suggest that communication should be cold or distant. Emotion, warmth, and storytelling all have their place. The key difference is intentionality. Strategic communicators decide when to elaborate and when to simplify. They adjust their language to the needs of the moment rather than speaking without direction.

Intentional speech increases effectiveness.

Precision also prevents manipulation. When someone expresses themselves clearly, it becomes difficult for others to twist their meaning or misrepresent their intentions. Careful wording creates a record that accurately reflects what was said. This protection becomes particularly important in professional, political, or legal environments.

Clear language protects truth.

Another aspect of this law involves listening. Effective speakers are often exceptional listeners. By paying close attention to what others say, they identify the real concerns beneath the conversation. When they respond, their words address the core issue rather than superficial distractions.

Listening guides precision.

Over time, disciplined communication transforms how others perceive you. When people notice that your statements are thoughtful and purposeful, they begin to take them seriously. Meetings become quieter when you begin speaking. Conversations become more attentive. Others recognize that your words carry meaning rather than noise.

Influence grows through restraint.

Ultimately, speaking with precision means respecting the power of language. Words can inspire cooperation, resolve conflicts, clarify ideas, and guide decisions. But when used carelessly, they can create misunderstanding, tension, and unnecessary conflict.

The strategic individual treats language as a tool of construction, not decoration.

Because in many situations, the person who speaks the least often says the most.

Principle of Law 15

Let your words be deliberate, clear, and purposeful.

Speak when your words improve the conversation.

Remain silent when they do not.

Strategic Training Drill, Law 15

Develop disciplined communication.

Pause briefly before responding in important conversations.

Remove unnecessary explanations when making a point.

Practice listening fully before speaking.

Choose words that express ideas clearly rather than impressively.

Ask yourself regularly:

Do my words clarify the situation or complicate it?

Precision in speech creates credibility in thought.

Chapter Sixteen

Chapter 16 Build Strategic Alliances Without Losing Independence

No one builds influence entirely alone.

Human societies operate through networks of cooperation. Businesses grow through partnerships. communities grow through shared effort. movements grow through alliances between individuals who recognize common interests. Because of this, the ability to form relationships is essential for progress.

Yet alliances contain a hidden danger.

When partnerships are formed without clear boundaries, independence can gradually disappear. One party becomes dependent on the approval, resources, or direction of another. Decisions begin to reflect the priorities of the stronger partner rather than the original purpose of the relationship. What began as cooperation can slowly transform into control.

Strategic alliances require balance.

The disciplined strategist understands that collaboration should strengthen both sides without allowing either side to dominate the other. This balance begins with clarity of purpose. Before entering any partnership, one must understand their own mission, principles, and limits. Without this clarity, alliances can pull individuals away from their original objectives.

Purpose protects independence.

Strong alliances are built on mutual benefit. Each participant contributes something valuable that the other recognizes. One partner may provide knowledge. Another may provide resources. Another may provide access to networks or opportunities. When contributions are balanced, the relationship remains cooperative rather than hierarchical.

Mutual benefit sustains cooperation.

However, strategic individuals remain aware that alliances are not permanent guarantees. Circumstances change. Interests evolve. People adjust their priorities as environments shift. For this reason, wise individuals maintain the ability to function independently even while cooperating with others.

Independence preserves freedom of movement.

Another important aspect of alliances is reputation. Individuals known for integrity and reliability attract stronger partners. When people trust that someone keeps their commitments and communicates honestly, they feel more comfortable entering collaborative relationships. Trust becomes the foundation that allows alliances to function smoothly.

Trust multiplies opportunity.

But trust does not eliminate the need for awareness. Strategic thinkers observe how partners behave under pressure. They watch how decisions are made when interests conflict. These moments reveal whether an alliance is built on genuine respect or temporary convenience.

Character reveals itself in difficulty.

Maintaining independence within alliances also requires personal discipline. It means continuing to develop your own skills, networks, and resources even while cooperating with others. When individuals rely entirely on a single relationship for success, they become vulnerable to shifts in that relationship. Maintaining independent capacity prevents this vulnerability.

Self-reliance strengthens alliances.

Another important principle is transparency of expectations. Many partnerships fail because assumptions were never discussed openly. Each side may imagine a different outcome, a different level of commitment, or a different distribution of benefits. When expectations remain unclear, misunderstandings eventually arise.

Clear agreements prevent confusion.

Strategic alliances also involve respect for boundaries. Healthy partnerships allow each participant to maintain their identity and direction. They cooperate where interests align and remain independent where they differ. This flexibility prevents unnecessary conflict and preserves long-term cooperation.

Respect sustains partnerships.

Over time, individuals who master this law become skilled network builders. They understand how to bring people together around shared goals while allowing each participant to maintain their own strength. Instead of creating dependency, they create collaboration that benefits everyone involved.

Collaboration expands influence.

These individuals also recognize when alliances have reached their natural conclusion. Not every partnership must last forever. When interests diverge or objectives change, the wise strategist transitions respectfully rather than forcing a relationship to continue beyond its usefulness.

Graceful exits preserve reputation.

Ultimately, strategic alliances function best when they are based on shared purpose rather than emotional obligation. When individuals cooperate because their goals align, their efforts reinforce one another. When those goals shift, each participant retains the ability to move forward independently.

Freedom remains intact.

Because the strongest alliances are not chains.

They are bridges.

Principle of Law 16

Build partnerships that strengthen your mission.

But never surrender the independence that allows you to pursue it.

Strategic Training Drill, Law 16

Strengthen your alliance strategy:

Clarify your mission before entering partnerships.

Seek collaborators whose goals align with yours.

Maintain your own skills and resources even while cooperating.

Establish expectations clearly at the beginning of agreements.

Ask yourself regularly:

Does this alliance strengthen my purpose or replace it?

The best alliances increase your reach without reducing your freedom.

Chapter Seventeen

PART III SOCIAL WARFARE

PART III SOCIAL WARFARE

LAW 17 Pay Attention to the Children of Power, Not Power Itself

Human Relationship Power Moves

The previous section focused on building credibility and authority.

This section explores something even more complex:

Power within human relationships.

Many people focus only on visible leaders, executives, politicians, public figures, or authority figures. Yet history repeatedly shows that the individuals surrounding those leaders often hold tremendous influence over decisions, opportunities, and outcomes.

Law 17 begins with understanding how influence moves through people.

LAW 17

Pay Attention to the Children of Power, Not Power Itself

Power rarely travels alone.

When people think about influence, they often focus on the individual who holds the official title or position of authority. They study the leader, the executive, the politician, or the public figure. But those who study power closely discover something important: the visible authority figure is only part of the structure.

Behind every influential individual exists a surrounding circle.

This circle may include assistants, advisors, protégés, relatives, trusted employees, long-time friends, or rising figures within the organization. These individuals interact with the leader regularly, influence conversations privately, and often shape decisions before they ever become public.

They are the children of power.

In many cases, these individuals reveal more about the direction of power than the leader themselves. Leaders may appear stable in public, but their influence gradually transfers to those they trust most. When someone is repeatedly given responsibility, access, and visibility within an organization, it often signals that they are being prepared for greater influence.

Observation reveals succession.

History provides countless examples of this pattern. Political leaders rely on advisors who eventually become leaders themselves. Business executives mentor successors who later guide the organization. Cultural figures develop protégés who continue their influence into the next generation. In each case, the individuals closest to power become its future carriers.

Future power grows quietly.

Those who understand this law study these relationships carefully. Instead of focusing only on the person currently holding authority, they observe who that person trusts. They notice who receives private meetings, who is asked to represent the leader publicly, and who is given increasing responsibility over time.

These signals reveal emerging influence.

Another reason to study the children of power is access. Leaders often protect their time and limit direct interaction with others. However, the individuals surrounding them frequently serve as the gateway to those interactions. Secretaries schedule meetings. Advisors filter information. Assistants determine priorities. These roles may appear secondary, but they influence which voices reach the leader and which do not.

Gateways control flow.

By understanding these relationships, strategic individuals navigate environments more effectively. Instead of attempting to confront authority directly, they build respectful relationships with those who help shape that authority's decisions. This approach is not manipulation; it is awareness of how human systems actually operate.

Influence moves through networks.

Another important insight is that the children of power often reveal the character of the leader themselves. Leaders tend to trust individuals who reflect their values, priorities, and judgment. By observing the behavior and attitudes of those closest to power, one can often understand the deeper principles guiding the leader's decisions.

Character reveals itself through association.

At times, these individuals may eventually surpass the influence of the leader they serve. Protégés gain experience through proximity to authority. They observe decision-making processes, learn institutional structures, and develop their own networks while operating under the protection of an established leader. When the time comes for transition, they are often the most prepared to step forward.

Preparation happens quietly.

Recognizing this law allows individuals to see influence developing long before it becomes visible to the public. While others focus on the current hierarchy, the observant strategist notices where future authority is forming. By understanding these dynamics early, they position themselves intelligently within evolving networks of power.

Awareness becomes advantage.

However, this law must be practiced with integrity. Relationships should never be formed purely for opportunistic gain. Genuine respect, professionalism, and cooperation create stronger connections than calculated flattery. Strategic awareness simply allows individuals to understand the environment they are operating within.

Respect sustains influence.

Over time, individuals who practice this awareness become skilled observers of human systems. They recognize that power is rarely static. It flows through relationships, mentorships, and networks of trust. By observing these movements carefully, they develop a clearer understanding of where influence is heading.

And those who understand where influence is going are better prepared for what comes next.

Because power rarely appears suddenly.

It grows quietly through those who stand beside it.

Principle of Law 17

Study those closest to power.

They often reveal where influence is moving long before others notice.

Strategic Training Drill, Law 17

Develop awareness of influence networks:

Observe who trusted leaders rely on most frequently.

Notice who receives increasing responsibility over time.

Build respectful relationships with individuals across all levels of an organization.

Pay attention to mentorship relationships and emerging successors.

Ask yourself regularly:

Who is learning from today's leaders and what role might they play tomorrow?

Understanding influence requires studying not only leaders, but the people who stand beside them.

Chapter Eighteen

Chapter 18 Identify Gatekeepers Early

Access is often controlled by those who appear least powerful.

Many people believe opportunities are decided solely by those with visible authority, the executives, directors, politicians, or leaders whose names appear at the top of an organization. But in practice, access to those individuals is often controlled by others whose roles seem less significant.

These individuals act as gatekeepers.

A gatekeeper is someone who controls the flow of information, introductions, opportunities, or resources within a system. They may be assistants, coordinators, administrators, advisors, managers, editors, recruiters, or trusted intermediaries. Their job places them in the position of determining who receives access and who does not.

Gatekeepers influence pathways.

Because they operate behind the scenes, many people overlook their importance. They focus their attention entirely on reaching the visible authority figure. Yet without the cooperation of the gatekeeper, that access may never occur. The gatekeeper filters requests, schedules meetings, and determines which voices reach the decision-maker.

Access often begins with them.

Strategic individuals recognize this reality early. Instead of ignoring gatekeepers or treating them as obstacles, they approach them with respect and professionalism. They understand that the gatekeeper's perception can influence whether opportunities are granted or delayed.

Respect opens doors.

Gatekeepers also possess valuable information about how systems operate. Because they manage communication and logistics, they often understand the priorities, schedules, and preferences of those in authority. This knowledge allows them to guide interactions effectively. When treated respectfully, they may share insights that help others navigate the environment successfully.

Information is influence.

Another reason gatekeepers are powerful is trust. Leaders frequently rely on gatekeepers because they need someone dependable to organize their time and manage requests. Over time, this trust grows. A gatekeeper who has proven reliable may gain significant influence over how information reaches the leader.

Trusted intermediaries shape decisions.

For this reason, the way someone treats gatekeepers often reflects their character. Individuals who show courtesy only toward those with visible power reveal opportunistic behavior. In contrast, those who treat everyone with dignity demonstrate professionalism and emotional intelligence.

Character is revealed in everyday interactions.

Understanding this law also encourages awareness of hierarchy beyond titles. In many environments, the official structure tells only part of the story. Informal influence often flows through individuals who connect different parts of the organization. These connectors may not have impressive titles, but they facilitate communication and cooperation between powerful individuals.

Connections move systems.

Strategic thinkers therefore observe carefully when entering a new environment. They identify who organizes meetings, who coordinates communication, and who is consulted before decisions are finalized. These individuals often function as gatekeepers even if their role is not formally described that way.

Observation reveals structure.

Once identified, relationships with gatekeepers should be approached authentically. Genuine courtesy, appreciation, and professionalism create stronger connections than calculated attempts to gain favor. Gatekeepers quickly recognize insincerity because they interact with many individuals seeking access.

Authenticity builds trust.

Another advantage of understanding gatekeepers is efficiency. Instead of wasting time navigating unclear processes, individuals who build respectful relationships with these intermediaries often learn the most effective pathways to accomplish their goals. Gatekeepers can explain procedures, clarify expectations, and prevent misunderstandings.

Guidance accelerates progress.

Over time, individuals who respect gatekeepers develop reputations as cooperative and thoughtful collaborators. This reputation improves the likelihood that their requests will be considered seriously and handled efficiently.

Professional respect multiplies opportunity.

Ultimately, the lesson of this law is simple: power rarely operates in isolation. It functions through networks of people performing different roles. By recognizing and respecting those roles, individuals gain a clearer understanding of how influence flows within complex systems.

Because sometimes the person who decides whether you enter the room

is more important than the person speaking inside it.

Principle of Law 18

Recognize and respect the individuals who control access.

They often influence outcomes more than their titles suggest.

Strategic Training Drill, Law 18

Strengthen your awareness of gatekeepers:

Identify who manages communication and scheduling within organizations.

Treat every role with consistent respect and professionalism.

Observe who others consult before important decisions.

Build genuine relationships with those who coordinate systems.

Ask yourself regularly:

Who controls access within this environment?

Understanding gatekeepers reveals how systems truly operate.

Chapter Nineteen

Chapter 19 Make Allies Without Being Owned by Them

Allies expand influence.

No individual succeeds entirely alone. Throughout history, progress has been achieved through cooperation between people whose goals align. Partnerships allow individuals to combine knowledge, resources, networks, and perspectives in ways that produce stronger outcomes than isolated effort.

Yet alliances contain a subtle danger.

When relationships are formed without maintaining independence, an ally can gradually become a source of control. Decisions begin to revolve around maintaining the alliance rather than advancing the original mission. The partnership becomes an obligation instead of a strategic collaboration.

Strategic alliances must strengthen freedom, not replace it.

The disciplined individual understands that alliances should exist because of shared interests, not dependency. Two individuals or groups cooperate because their objectives align. Each participant benefits from the partnership while retaining the ability to operate independently if circumstances change.

Mutual strength creates stable alliances.

A partnership built on dependency often becomes unstable over time. When one side relies completely on the other for resources, approval, or direction, the balance of power shifts. The stronger party may begin shaping decisions according to their own priorities. Eventually the dependent partner loses the freedom to act according to their original vision.

Dependency invites control.

For this reason, strategic thinkers develop their own capabilities before entering alliances. They cultivate skills, networks, and resources that allow them to stand independently. When individuals possess their own strength, alliances become partnerships of equals rather than relationships of necessity.

Strength attracts stronger allies.

Another essential element of healthy alliances is clarity of purpose. Partnerships should be formed around clearly understood goals. When both sides know what they are working toward, cooperation becomes focused and efficient. Without clarity, alliances may drift into confusion or conflict as expectations diverge.

Shared direction strengthens cooperation.

Communication also plays a crucial role. Honest dialogue prevents misunderstandings about responsibilities, contributions, and benefits. Strategic individuals express expectations openly and listen carefully to the perspectives of their partners. This transparency builds trust while protecting both sides from hidden assumptions.

Clear communication sustains alliances.

At the same time, maintaining independence requires emotional discipline. Strong partnerships often create loyalty and personal attachment. While loyalty can strengthen cooperation, excessive emotional dependence can cloud judgment. Strategic individuals remain appreciative of their allies while remembering that alliances exist to serve shared purposes.

Purpose must remain central.

Another advantage of maintaining independence is flexibility. Conditions change constantly. Markets evolve, political environments shift, and organizational priorities transform. Individuals who rely entirely on a single alliance may struggle to adapt when those conditions change. Independent capacity allows someone to adjust strategies while preserving valuable relationships.

Flexibility protects progress.

There is also dignity in balanced alliances. When both partners respect each other's independence, cooperation becomes more genuine. Each side participates because they value the partnership, not because they are trapped within it. This mutual respect strengthens trust and encourages long-term collaboration.

Respect creates lasting alliances.

Strategic thinkers also understand that alliances do not require complete agreement. Two parties may cooperate effectively on certain goals while maintaining different perspectives in other areas. This flexibility allows partnerships to function without forcing individuals to compromise their principles.

Cooperation does not require surrender.

Over time, individuals who practice this law develop networks of collaborators rather than chains of dependency. They build relationships with people who respect their independence and contribute to shared progress. These networks create opportunities, exchange knowledge, and support innovation without restricting freedom.

Networks multiply influence.

Ultimately, the purpose of alliances is expansion. They allow individuals to accomplish more together than they could alone. But the moment an alliance begins limiting independence rather than strengthening it, its strategic value diminishes.

Because the strongest allies walk beside you.

They do not stand above you.

Principle of Law 19

Build alliances that expand your mission.

But never surrender the independence that allows you to pursue it.

Strategic Training Drill, Law 19

Develop healthy alliances.

Clarify your mission before entering partnerships.

Seek allies whose goals align with yours.

Maintain your own skills, resources, and networks.

Communicate expectations openly at the beginning of collaborations.

Ask yourself regularly:

Does this alliance strengthen my freedom or reduce it?

The best alliances create cooperation without creating control.

Chapter Twenty

Chapter 20 Use Words as Architecture

Language does more than communicate ideas.

It builds frameworks through which people understand reality.

Every society operates through shared language. Laws are written with words. Institutions are defined with words. Narratives about history, identity, and power are constructed through words. Because of this, language does not merely describe the world, it helps shape the way people perceive it.

Words build mental structures.

When someone chooses language carefully, they influence how others interpret events, ideas, and relationships. A single phrase can change the emotional tone of an entire conversation. A well-constructed argument can reshape public opinion. Even the labels applied to people or situations can determine whether something is viewed as acceptable, controversial, or unjust.

Language organizes perception.

For example, describing an action as "necessary reform" creates a different reaction than describing the same action as "radical change." Both phrases may refer to the same policy, but the emotional response they produce is different. This demonstrates how language functions as architecture: it builds the framework within which ideas are evaluated.

Words create context.

Strategic communicators understand this power. They do not speak randomly or reactively. Instead, they consider how each phrase contributes to the larger understanding of the situation. They frame ideas in ways that highlight their purpose and clarify their meaning.

Framing guides interpretation.

Another dimension of linguistic architecture is narrative. Humans naturally understand the world through stories. When events are organized into narratives, people can see cause, effect, conflict, and resolution. Those who control narrative language often shape how history itself is remembered.

Narratives influence memory.

This principle explains why social movements, institutions, and governments devote significant attention to messaging. The words used to describe a problem influence how the public understands the solution. If a challenge is described in a certain way, people begin searching for answers within that framework.

Language directs attention.

Strategic individuals also understand that language can either divide or unify. Certain phrases emphasize conflict and difference. Others emphasize shared purpose and cooperation. The words chosen during important conversations can determine whether participants feel defensive or collaborative.

Language shapes relationships.

Another aspect of this law involves clarity. Complex ideas often lose influence when expressed with confusing language. When ideas are explained in clear and accessible terms, they become easier for others to understand and share. Clear language spreads more easily because it invites participation rather than confusion.

Clarity multiplies influence.

However, using language as architecture requires responsibility. Words can inspire progress, but they can also manipulate or mislead. Strategic individuals therefore use language to clarify truth rather than obscure it. They aim to construct understanding rather than confusion.

Integrity strengthens communication.

Listening also plays an essential role in linguistic architecture. By paying attention to how others describe their experiences and concerns, communicators gain insight into how those individuals understand the world. Effective responses then build bridges between perspectives rather than ignoring them.

Listening strengthens connection.

Over time, individuals who master this law become skilled at shaping conversations constructively. They know how to frame ideas so that others can understand their significance. They know when to simplify complex issues and when to explain them in depth. Their language becomes a tool for building clarity rather than confusion.

Their words create structure.

Because when language is used intentionally, it does more than describe reality.

It helps construct it.

Principle of Law 20

Choose language that clarifies reality and guides understanding.

Words are not only communication.

They are architecture for thought.

Strategic Training Drill, Law 20

Develop disciplined language awareness:

Notice how different words change the tone of a message.

Practice explaining complex ideas in clear language.

Frame problems in ways that highlight constructive solutions.

Listen carefully to the language others use to describe their experiences.

Ask yourself regularly:

What kind of understanding are my words building?

Every sentence contributes to the structure through which people interpret the world.

Choose that structure wisely.

Chapter Twenty-One

Chapter 21 Protect Your Reputation Like a Nation Protects Borders

Your reputation is your social territory.

Just as a nation protects its borders to preserve sovereignty, individuals must protect their reputation to preserve influence. Reputation represents the accumulated perception others hold about your character, reliability, and capability. It travels ahead of you into rooms you have not yet entered and influences how people respond to you before you speak.

Reputation precedes presence.

When someone is known for honesty, discipline, and competence, their reputation creates trust before any interaction occurs. People expect integrity because past behavior has demonstrated it repeatedly. This expectation opens doors, strengthens partnerships, and encourages cooperation.

Trust expands opportunity.

However, reputation is also fragile. It is built slowly through consistent behavior but can be damaged quickly by a single careless action. Words spoken impulsively, promises broken, or conduct that contradicts previously demonstrated principles can create doubt in the minds of observers.

Doubt weakens influence.

Because reputation functions as social memory, individuals remember patterns rather than isolated moments. If someone repeatedly demonstrates reliability, occasional mistakes may be forgiven. But if negative behavior becomes a pattern, reputation shifts accordingly.

Patterns define identity.

Protecting reputation therefore requires consistent discipline. Strategic individuals recognize that every interaction contributes to the larger narrative others construct about them. The way they communicate, respond to challenges, treat others, and fulfill commitments all become evidence that shapes perception.

Conduct writes reputation.

Another aspect of protecting reputation involves managing misunderstandings. In complex environments, rumors and incomplete information can spread quickly. Strategic individuals address inaccuracies calmly and clearly before they grow into larger misconceptions.

Clarification protects truth.

At the same time, not every criticism requires response. Sometimes engaging with accusations only amplifies them. Strategic individuals evaluate whether silence or clarification better protects their reputation. This judgment requires patience and awareness of context.

Discernment preserves dignity.

Reputation also functions as a shield. When individuals have demonstrated integrity over time, others are more likely to defend them when challenges arise. Colleagues who know their character may question negative claims because those claims contradict previous experience.

Trust defends character.

This protective effect becomes particularly valuable in environments where competition exists. When disagreements occur, reputation helps observers determine whom they believe. A person known for fairness and reliability begins with credibility that others must earn.

Credibility strengthens authority.

Another important element of reputation management is consistency across environments. Individuals who behave with integrity only in public settings but differently in private interactions eventually expose contradictions. Over time, these inconsistencies erode trust.

Integrity requires alignment.

Strategic individuals therefore treat every interaction as part of the same ethical framework. They maintain similar standards whether they are speaking to colleagues, subordinates, leaders, or strangers. This consistency creates a stable reputation that others recognize as genuine.

Consistency builds credibility.

Reputation also influences future opportunities. People prefer to collaborate with individuals whose past behavior suggests reliability and professionalism. When someone's reputation reflects competence and respect, others feel confident inviting them into meaningful roles and responsibilities.

Opportunity follows reputation.

Over time, a strong reputation becomes a form of personal sovereignty. It allows individuals to move through environments with confidence because their character has already been demonstrated. Their name becomes associated with certain standards, and those standards shape how others interact with them.

Character becomes currency.

Ultimately, protecting reputation requires awareness of how actions contribute to long-term perception. Strategic individuals do not merely think about the immediate effect of their behavior. They consider how that behavior will be remembered later and what story it contributes to the narrative others construct.

Because reputation is not only what people say about you today.

It is the story they repeat tomorrow.

Principle of Law 21

Your reputation is your social border.

Protect it carefully, because once trust is broken, influence becomes difficult to restore.

Strategic Training Drill, Law 21

Strengthen your reputation intentionally:

Keep commitments even when they become inconvenient.

Speak truthfully and avoid exaggeration.

Address misunderstandings calmly when necessary.

Maintain consistent standards across all interactions.

Ask yourself regularly:

What story does my behavior tell about my character?

Your reputation is the memory others carry of your integrity.

Guard it with discipline.

Chapter Twenty-Two

Chapter 22 Never Beg for Respect

Respect cannot be requested into existence.

When someone asks others to respect them, it often signals uncertainty about their own authority. Words alone rarely create genuine regard. Instead, respect develops from observable patterns of conduct, how someone behaves, how they respond to pressure, and how consistently they uphold their principles.

Respect is earned through behavior.

People instinctively observe how individuals carry themselves in different situations. When someone demonstrates calm discipline, fairness, reliability, and confidence, others begin to respond differently. They speak more thoughtfully around them. They consider their opinions more carefully. They acknowledge their presence without needing to be reminded.

Authority emerges naturally.

Begging for respect has the opposite effect. When someone repeatedly demands recognition or insists that others treat them a certain way, it can weaken the perception of their confidence. Observers may feel that the person is attempting to compensate for something that should already be evident.

Confidence speaks quietly.

This does not mean that disrespect should be tolerated. Strategic individuals set clear boundaries when necessary. They address inappropriate behavior calmly and directly. However, their response focuses on maintaining standards rather than seeking approval.

Boundaries communicate dignity.

Another important dimension of respect is self-respect. People tend to treat others according to how those individuals treat themselves. Someone who compromises their principles for convenience or approval may find that others gradually lower their expectations of them. In contrast, individuals who maintain their values even when it is difficult often inspire greater regard.

Consistency commands respect.

Self-respect also influences decision-making. When individuals understand their own worth, they are less likely to accept conditions that undermine their dignity or purpose. They choose environments, relationships, and opportunities that align with their standards rather than simply pursuing approval.

Choice reflects confidence.

Respect also grows through competence. When someone repeatedly produces high-quality work, fulfills commitments, and contributes meaningful solutions, observers recognize the value they bring. This recognition often transforms into respect because people trust the individual's ability and judgment.

Competence strengthens credibility.

Another element of respect involves composure. When individuals remain calm during conflict or pressure, they demonstrate control over their emotions and reactions. This composure signals maturity and reliability, qualities that others often associate with leadership.

Composure inspires confidence.

It is also important to understand that respect does not require universal approval. Some individuals may disagree with your ideas or decisions. However, even disagreement can coexist with respect when someone demonstrates integrity and consistency.

Respect does not require agreement.

Over time, individuals who follow this law develop a presence that commands attention without demanding it. Their conduct communicates their standards clearly. Others learn how to interact with them because their boundaries and expectations are consistent.

Presence becomes authority.

Ultimately, respect grows from alignment between character and action. When individuals live according to principles they genuinely believe in, their behavior reflects authenticity. Authenticity encourages trust, and trust strengthens respect.

Because people recognize sincerity more easily than performance.

The strongest form of respect does not come from titles, popularity, or demands.

It comes from character that remains steady regardless of circumstance.

Principle of Law 22

Respect is not requested.

It is demonstrated through consistent conduct, integrity, and confidence.

Strategic Training Drill, Law 22

Strengthen authentic respect:

Maintain your principles even when it is inconvenient.

Set clear boundaries when necessary without hostility.

Focus on competence and reliability in your work.

Practice calm composure during disagreements or pressure.

Ask yourself regularly:

Does my behavior reflect the respect I expect from others?

True respect grows from the example you set.

Chapter Twenty-Three

Chapter 23 Read the Subtext, Not the Text

Words rarely tell the full story.

In professional, political, and social environments, people often communicate indirectly. Politeness, diplomacy, caution, or strategy may prevent individuals from stating their true thoughts openly. Instead, meaning appears beneath the surface of the conversation.

This hidden meaning is called subtext.

Subtext refers to the underlying message behind what someone says. While the text represents the literal words spoken, the subtext reflects intention, emotion, or strategy. Understanding this difference allows individuals to interpret conversations more accurately.

Listening becomes observation.

For example, someone may say, "That's an interesting idea," while their tone and body language suggest doubt or hesitation. Another person might say, "We should discuss that later," when they actually mean they prefer to avoid the topic entirely. In these situations, the literal statement does not fully represent the speaker's intention.

Meaning exists beneath the words.

Strategic individuals therefore pay attention to more than language alone. They observe tone of voice, timing of responses, facial expressions, and patterns of behavior. These signals often reveal more about someone's true position than the sentence itself.

Context reveals intention.

Another important indicator of subtext is inconsistency between words and actions. When someone repeatedly promises cooperation but delays progress, their behavior may communicate reluctance. When someone praises an idea publicly but avoids supporting it privately, their actions reveal their true perspective.

Behavior clarifies meaning.

Understanding subtext also requires awareness of social dynamics. Individuals may soften criticism to maintain harmony, avoid confrontation, or protect relationships. Others may disguise ambition through modest language while pursuing significant influence behind the scenes.

Diplomacy masks strategy.

Those who fail to recognize subtext may misunderstand situations entirely. They might accept statements at face value without recognizing the deeper implications. As a result, they may misjudge alliances, overlook warnings, or misinterpret opportunities.

Literal thinking can limit awareness.

However, interpreting subtext should not lead to suspicion of every statement. Effective observers balance attentiveness with fairness. They consider context, history, and patterns rather than jumping to conclusions based on isolated remarks.

Judgment requires patience.

Another advantage of recognizing subtext is improved communication. When individuals understand what others truly mean, they can respond more thoughtfully. They address the underlying concern rather than the surface statement. This ability often leads to clearer conversations and more effective problem-solving.

Insight improves dialogue.

Reading subtext also helps individuals recognize unspoken opportunities. Sometimes others express interest indirectly to avoid appearing too eager. Observing these subtle signals allows strategic individuals to recognize possibilities that might otherwise remain unnoticed.

Opportunity often whispers.

Over time, individuals who develop this awareness become skilled interpreters of social environments. They understand when encouragement is genuine, when hesitation signals concern, and when enthusiasm masks uncertainty. This insight allows them to respond with greater precision and confidence.

Understanding grows deeper.

Ultimately, the ability to read subtext strengthens emotional intelligence. It allows individuals to navigate complex conversations with sensitivity and awareness. By listening not only to words but also to context and behavior, they gain a clearer understanding of what others truly intend.

Because in many situations, the most important part of communication is not what is said.

It is what is meant.

Principle of Law 23

Listen beyond the words.

True meaning often appears in tone, behavior, and context rather than in the sentence itself.

Strategic Training Drill, Law 23

Strengthen your ability to read subtext:

Observe tone of voice and body language during conversations.

Compare what people say with what they consistently do.

Consider the broader context surrounding each discussion.

Avoid reacting immediately, allow patterns to reveal themselves.

Ask yourself regularly:

What message might exist beneath the words being spoken?

Understanding subtext allows you to navigate complex environments with greater clarity.

Chapter Twenty-Four

Chapter 24 Learn When to Withdraw Completely

Presence is powerful.

But absence can be even more powerful.

Many individuals believe that strength means remaining constantly engaged in every conflict, debate, or situation. They respond to every criticism, argue every disagreement, and attempt to prove their point in every conversation. While this may appear assertive, it often drains energy and escalates conflicts unnecessarily.

Constant engagement weakens focus.

Strategic individuals understand that not every situation deserves their attention. Some conflicts exist only to provoke reaction. Others drain time without producing meaningful progress. In these situations, continuing to participate may benefit the other party more than it benefits you.

Disengagement becomes strategy.

Withdrawal does not mean surrender. It means recognizing when a situation no longer contributes to your purpose. By stepping away, individuals preserve their energy, protect their reputation, and avoid becoming entangled in conflicts that offer little value.

Energy is a limited resource.

Another advantage of strategic withdrawal is perspective. When individuals remain constantly immersed in tension or disagreement, their judgment can become clouded by emotion. Stepping back creates distance that allows clearer thinking. With distance, individuals can evaluate the situation objectively and determine whether further engagement is worthwhile.

Distance restores clarity.

Withdrawal also interrupts negative patterns. In some conflicts, the opposing party may rely on continued reaction to maintain momentum. When one side refuses to participate, the cycle often loses energy. The absence of reaction removes the fuel that sustains the conflict.

Silence disrupts escalation.

Strategic absence can also increase influence in certain situations. When someone who normally contributes thoughtful ideas suddenly withdraws from discussion, others may begin to notice the absence. Questions arise about why they are no longer participating. This shift in attention can highlight the value of their perspective more clearly than constant presence.

Absence reveals value.

Another reason to withdraw at times is personal renewal. Continuous engagement with demanding environments can exhaust mental and emotional resources. Taking time to step back allows individuals to rest, reflect, and return with renewed clarity and strength.

Recovery strengthens resilience.

However, withdrawal must be practiced with discernment. Avoiding responsibility or abandoning commitments can damage reputation. Strategic withdrawal applies specifically to situations that are unproductive, destructive, or misaligned with one's goals.

Discernment protects integrity.

Those who master this law learn to distinguish between battles that matter and those that do not. They invest their attention where it produces meaningful results. When circumstances become unproductive, they step away without hostility or explanation, preserving their dignity and focus.

Purpose guides engagement.

This discipline also demonstrates confidence. Individuals who constantly defend themselves may appear insecure about their position. Those who withdraw calmly signal that they are secure enough not to react to every challenge.

Confidence requires restraint.

Over time, strategic withdrawal becomes a powerful form of self-governance. It allows individuals to choose where their energy will be invested rather than allowing circumstances to dictate their attention. By focusing only on situations aligned with their mission, they maintain clarity and effectiveness.

Choice preserves strength.

Ultimately, influence is not determined by how often someone speaks or engages. It is determined by the impact of the moments they choose to participate.

Because sometimes the strongest move is not to push harder.

It is to step away.

Principle of Law 24

Not every conflict deserves your attention.

Withdraw from situations that waste energy or distract from your purpose.

Strategic Training Drill, Law 24

Practice disciplined withdrawal:

Identify conflicts that produce no meaningful progress.

Step back from conversations that exist only to provoke reaction.

Preserve your energy for situations aligned with your goals.

Use distance to evaluate situations with greater clarity.

Ask yourself regularly:

Is my participation improving this situation or prolonging it?

Strategic absence protects strength.

Chapter Twenty-Five

PART IV ECONOMIC WARFARE: POWER THROUGH RESOURCES

We now begin a new phase of the book:

PART IV ECONOMIC WARFARE: POWER THROUGH RESOURCES

LAW 25 Own Something or Be Owned

Money, Ownership, and Strategic Independence

The previous section explored social power and influence.

Now we shift to something even more foundational.

Economic power.

History consistently shows that communities and individuals who control resources possess greater independence than those who rely entirely on others for survival. Economic strength allows people to make decisions according to their values rather than according to necessity.

The first law of this section addresses the core principle of economic sovereignty.

LAW 25

Own Something or Be Owned

Ownership determines independence.

Throughout history, the ability to own property, land, intellectual creations, or productive businesses has shaped the balance of power within societies. Those who control resources possess the ability to direct their own decisions. Those who depend entirely on others for access to resources must often accept conditions imposed by those who own them.

Control follows ownership.

Ownership provides stability because it creates a foundation that does not disappear with changing circumstances. A job may end, an organization may restructure, and economic conditions may fluctuate. However, assets that are owned, whether land, a business, or intellectual property, continue to exist beyond temporary changes.

Assets create continuity.

This principle does not suggest that employment or collaboration lack value. Many people begin their careers by working within organizations where they develop skills and experience. These opportunities can be valuable stepping stones. However, relying solely on employment without developing ownership can limit long-term independence.

Employment provides income.

Ownership provides leverage.

Ownership also creates opportunity for growth. When individuals control an asset, the value of that asset can increase over time. Land may appreciate. Businesses may expand. Intellectual property may generate royalties or influence. These forms of growth create economic momentum that extends beyond a single paycheck.

Growth multiplies resources.

Another advantage of ownership is decision-making authority. Owners determine how resources are used, how profits are reinvested, and how future opportunities are pursued. This authority allows individuals to align economic activity with their goals rather than adapting constantly to the priorities of others.

Authority directs outcomes.

However, ownership requires responsibility. Assets must be managed carefully to remain productive. Businesses require planning, discipline, and adaptability. Intellectual property requires protection and strategic use. Those who pursue ownership must also develop the knowledge and discipline necessary to sustain it.

Responsibility sustains value.

Another important aspect of ownership is diversification. Relying on a single asset or income source can create vulnerability. Strategic individuals therefore develop multiple forms of ownership over time. These may include investments, business interests, creative works, or other assets that provide financial stability from different directions.

Diversification protects independence.

Ownership also influences how individuals view time. Instead of working only for immediate income, owners often focus on long-term value creation. They invest effort into projects that may grow gradually but eventually produce lasting returns. This perspective encourages patience and strategic planning.

Long-term thinking builds wealth.

Communities that emphasize ownership often develop stronger economic foundations. When businesses, property, and institutions are owned locally, resources circulate within the community rather than leaving it. This circulation creates employment, stability, and opportunity for future generations.

Ownership strengthens communities.

Yet ownership does not require vast wealth at the beginning. Many successful owners begin with small assets and expand gradually through discipline and reinvestment. The key is developing the habit of acquiring and maintaining productive assets over time.

Small ownership can grow into large ownership.

Ultimately, the choice between ownership and dependency shapes the direction of economic life. Individuals who pursue ownership gradually gain more control over their circumstances. Those who rely entirely on external systems remain vulnerable to decisions made by others.

Economic independence grows from what you control.

Because in every society, resources determine power.

And those who own the resources decide how they are used.

Principle of Law 25

Ownership creates independence.

Develop assets that allow you to shape your future rather than depend entirely on the decisions of others.

Strategic Training Drill, Law 25

Strengthen economic independence:

Identify opportunities to own productive assets.

Develop skills that allow you to create or manage those assets.

Reinvest income into ownership rather than consumption alone.

Diversify assets gradually to protect stability.

Ask yourself regularly:

What do I control that continues to produce value over time?

Ownership transforms effort into lasting influence.

Chapter Twenty-Six

Chapter 26 Build Personal Economic Insulation

Economic insulation creates stability.

In every economy, uncertainty exists. Markets fluctuate, organizations restructure, industries change, and unexpected events can alter financial circumstances quickly. Individuals who rely on a single source of income or a fragile financial structure often experience significant stress when these changes occur.

Economic insulation protects against these disruptions.

Economic insulation means creating layers of financial protection that allow you to maintain stability even when circumstances shift. Just as buildings are insulated to protect against temperature changes, individuals can create financial insulation to protect against economic shocks.

Protection creates resilience.

One of the most common forms of economic vulnerability is dependence on a single income source. When all financial stability depends on one employer, one client, or one opportunity, unexpected changes can create immediate hardship. Strategic individuals therefore seek to diversify their sources of income over time.

Multiple streams strengthen security.

Savings also play a critical role in insulation. Maintaining financial reserves allows individuals to handle emergencies without immediate crisis. These reserves provide time to make thoughtful decisions rather than reacting under pressure.

Time improves judgment.

Another layer of insulation involves managing debt carefully. Excessive debt can weaken financial independence because it requires constant payments regardless of changing circumstances. Strategic individuals evaluate debt carefully, distinguishing between obligations that support productive investment and those that create unnecessary financial strain.

Responsible borrowing protects flexibility.

Insurance and legal protections also contribute to economic insulation. Health insurance, property insurance, and other forms of risk management prevent unexpected events from creating overwhelming financial loss. While these protections require planning and expense, they often prevent far greater losses later.

Preparation reduces risk.

Another important aspect of economic insulation is skill development. Individuals whose knowledge and abilities remain valuable across multiple industries possess a form of economic protection.

When one opportunity disappears, their skills allow them to adapt to another.

Adaptability protects income.

Economic insulation also involves thoughtful spending habits. Individuals who align their expenses with their long-term priorities create financial breathing room. When spending grows beyond sustainable levels, even small disruptions can create major difficulties.

Discipline strengthens stability.

Investments provide another layer of insulation. Assets such as investments, businesses, or intellectual property can generate income independent of active labor. Over time, these assets contribute to financial resilience because they continue producing value even when personal circumstances change.

Assets extend security.

Another advantage of economic insulation is psychological stability. Financial stress often influences decision-making in unhealthy ways. Individuals facing immediate financial pressure may accept unfavorable conditions simply to resolve urgent problems. Economic insulation reduces this pressure by providing time and options.

Options strengthen freedom.

Communities also benefit when their members develop economic insulation. Individuals who possess financial stability can support others, invest in shared projects, and contribute to long-term community development. Economic security therefore strengthens both personal independence and collective progress.

Security supports cooperation.

Ultimately, building economic insulation is an act of foresight. It requires thinking beyond immediate needs and preparing for future uncertainty. While this preparation may require discipline and patience, it creates resilience that allows individuals to navigate changing circumstances with confidence.

Because stability is not accidental.

It is constructed intentionally.

Principle of Law 26

Economic insulation protects independence.

Create financial layers that allow you to remain stable even when circumstances change.

Strategic Training Drill, Law 26

Strengthen your economic insulation:

Develop multiple sources of income over time.

Maintain financial reserves for unexpected situations.

Manage debt carefully and avoid unnecessary obligations.

Invest in skills that remain valuable across changing industries.

Ask yourself regularly:

If one income source disappeared today, what would protect me?

Preparation transforms uncertainty into manageable risk.

Chapter Twenty-Seven

Chapter 27 Understand Institutional Bias and Organizational Algorithms

Modern systems often appear neutral.

Corporations, universities, financial institutions, and government agencies frequently present themselves as objective structures guided by policies, procedures, and measurable data. Decisions are often described as the result of standardized processes designed to ensure fairness.

However, systems are built by people.

Because humans design institutions, the systems they create often reflect their assumptions, experiences, and priorities. Over time, these assumptions become embedded in procedures, evaluation standards, and decision-making frameworks.

These embedded patterns can influence outcomes.

In modern environments, many organizations rely on algorithmic processes to assist decision-making. Algorithms may screen job applications, evaluate credit risk, recommend candidates for promotion, or determine access to services. While these systems are designed to increase efficiency, they often rely on historical data to make predictions.

Historical data can carry historical bias.

If past decisions within an institution reflected unequal access to opportunity, those patterns may become encoded in the data used by algorithms. When algorithms analyze this information, they may unintentionally reproduce the same patterns in future decisions. As a result, systems that appear neutral can sometimes perpetuate unequal outcomes.

Patterns repeat unless examined.

Understanding this reality allows individuals to navigate institutions more strategically. Instead of assuming that outcomes are always purely merit-based or purely biased, strategic thinkers examine how systems actually operate. They study evaluation criteria, promotion pathways, hiring processes, and decision-making structures.

Knowledge reveals patterns.

Another important aspect of institutional systems is networking. Many opportunities within organizations emerge not only from formal evaluation but also from relationships, mentorship, and visibility. Individuals who understand this dynamic actively build professional relationships that increase their awareness of opportunities and expectations.

Networks expand access.

Documentation also becomes essential in institutional environments. Maintaining records of work, achievements, and communication can provide clarity when questions arise regarding evaluation or advancement. Organized documentation helps ensure that contributions remain visible and verifiable.

Evidence strengthens credibility.

Strategic individuals also develop adaptability. When they recognize that a particular environment limits opportunity, they evaluate whether alternative paths may better align with their goals. This might involve seeking opportunities in different organizations, industries, or entrepreneurial ventures.

Flexibility preserves progress.

Education and skill development further strengthen independence. Individuals who continuously develop valuable skills increase their ability to move between opportunities rather than remaining confined within a single structure. This mobility reduces vulnerability to institutional limitations.

Skill creates mobility.

Another important strategy is collective awareness. When individuals share information about institutional processes and patterns, communities become better equipped to navigate those systems effectively. Transparency and knowledge exchange allow others to prepare for challenges and opportunities alike.

Shared knowledge strengthens communities.

It is also important to recognize that institutions evolve over time. Public awareness, legal frameworks, and internal reform efforts can influence how organizations operate. Individuals who understand both the strengths and weaknesses of institutions can contribute constructively to improving them.

Awareness supports progress.

Ultimately, understanding institutional systems provides clarity. It allows individuals to navigate complex environments with realistic expectations rather than assumptions. By studying patterns carefully, people can position themselves strategically while continuing to develop independence and opportunity.

Because systems influence outcomes.

But understanding systems increases the ability to navigate them effectively.

Principle of Law 27

Study how institutions actually operate.

Understanding patterns within systems allows you to navigate them with greater awareness and strategy.

Strategic Training Drill, Law 27

Develop institutional awareness:

Study how decisions are made within organizations.

Document your work, contributions, and achievements.

Build professional networks that expand access to information.

Continue developing skills that increase career mobility.

Ask yourself regularly:

Do I understand how this system truly operates?

Knowledge of systems transforms uncertainty into strategy.

Chapter Twenty-Eight

Chapter 28 Develop Multiple Streams of Identity, Not Just Income

Who you are shapes what you can earn.

Most people are taught to think about income as the primary measure of financial security. They pursue a single profession, develop expertise in one area, and rely on that identity to provide stability throughout their careers.

While specialization has advantages, relying on a single identity can also create vulnerability.

When someone defines themselves entirely by one role, a job title, profession, or industry, their opportunities become limited to the conditions of that role. If the industry changes, the company closes, or demand for that profession declines, the individual may struggle to adapt.

Identity influences opportunity.

Strategic individuals therefore develop multiple dimensions of identity over time. Instead of seeing themselves only as employees, they cultivate roles such as creator, investor, entrepreneur, mentor, or educator. Each identity opens different pathways for contribution and opportunity.

Diverse identities expand possibilities.

For example, someone may work as a professional in one field while also developing creative projects, consulting expertise, or educational content related to their knowledge. These additional identities allow them to generate opportunities that do not rely solely on their primary employment.

Multiple identities create flexibility.

Another advantage of identity diversification is intellectual growth. When individuals explore different domains of knowledge and skill, they often discover connections between fields that others overlook. These insights can lead to innovation, new business ideas, or unique career paths.

Cross-disciplinary thinking creates innovation.

Identity diversification also encourages long-term thinking. Individuals who develop multiple roles often view their work as part of a larger life mission rather than a single career path. This perspective encourages experimentation, continuous learning, and adaptability.

Adaptability strengthens resilience.

Another important benefit is independence. When someone has several professional identities, they gain greater control over their time and direction. They are less likely to feel trapped by a single role because other avenues remain available.

Choice strengthens freedom.

Modern technology has expanded opportunities for identity diversification. Digital platforms allow individuals to publish ideas, teach skills, create businesses, and collaborate globally. These tools make it possible to develop additional professional identities even while maintaining traditional employment.

Technology expands access.

However, developing multiple identities requires discipline. Attempting too many projects simultaneously can dilute focus. Strategic individuals therefore develop new identities gradually, allowing each one to mature before expanding further.

Growth requires patience.

Another important aspect of identity diversification is authenticity. Each role should reflect genuine interests and abilities rather than simply chasing trends. Authentic identities sustain motivation because they align with personal values and curiosity.

Authenticity fuels persistence.

Communities also benefit when individuals develop diverse identities. People who possess varied skills and perspectives contribute to innovation, mentorship, and economic growth within their networks. Diverse identities strengthen collective resilience.

Diversity strengthens communities.

Ultimately, developing multiple streams of identity transforms how individuals approach opportunity. Instead of waiting for opportunities to appear within a single role, they create opportunities across several domains of contribution.

Their identity becomes a platform for possibility.

Because economic strength is not only about how much you earn.

It is about how many ways you are capable of creating value.

Principle of Law 28

Expand your identity beyond a single role.

The more ways you can create value, the more opportunities you can generate.

Strategic Training Drill, Law 28

Strengthen identity diversification:

Identify skills or interests that could develop into additional professional roles.

Explore opportunities to teach, create, invest, or collaborate beyond your primary work.

Develop new identities gradually while maintaining focus and quality.

Use technology and networks to expand your reach.

Ask yourself regularly:

In how many ways can I create value for others?

Multiple identities create multiple pathways to opportunity.

Chapter Twenty-Nine

Chapter 29 Make Your Skills Portable

A skill that only works in one place is fragile.

Many individuals spend years developing expertise that functions only within a specific organization, company system, or narrow environment. While this specialization may bring short-term success, it can create vulnerability when circumstances change. If the organization restructures, closes, or replaces the position, the individual may discover that their expertise cannot easily transfer elsewhere.

Portability creates security.

Portable skills are abilities that remain valuable across industries, organizations, and geographic locations. These skills are not tied to one employer, one technology, or one system. Instead, they represent capabilities that can be applied in many different environments.

Versatility strengthens independence.

Examples of portable skills include communication, problem-solving, leadership, strategic thinking, negotiation, teaching, writing, technical literacy, and project management. These abilities can be applied in numerous fields because they support fundamental aspects of human cooperation and productivity.

Fundamental skills travel.

Strategic individuals intentionally cultivate these transferable abilities. They understand that industries evolve rapidly as technology advances and economic conditions change. By focusing on adaptable skills, they ensure that their knowledge remains valuable even when specific tools or procedures become outdated.

Adaptability protects relevance.

Another advantage of portable skills is mobility. Individuals with transferable abilities can move between roles, industries, or entrepreneurial ventures more easily than those whose knowledge is restricted to a single context. This mobility increases freedom of choice and reduces dependence on any one organization.

Mobility creates leverage.

Portable skills also enhance problem-solving capacity. Because these abilities apply across different situations, individuals who develop them learn to recognize patterns and apply solutions creatively. This flexibility allows them to contribute effectively in unfamiliar environments.

Experience broadens perspective.

Continuous learning plays an essential role in maintaining portability. Skills that were valuable in one era may require refinement as technology and methods evolve. Strategic individuals therefore treat education as an ongoing process rather than a one-time achievement.

Learning sustains relevance.

Another important aspect of portability is documentation. When individuals record their accomplishments, projects, and contributions, they create evidence of their abilities that can be demonstrated across different environments. Portfolios, certifications, and documented experience help translate skills into opportunities.

Proof supports credibility.

Communication also strengthens portability. Individuals who can explain their skills clearly to others make it easier for potential collaborators, employers, or partners to understand the value they bring. Clear articulation transforms experience into recognized expertise.

Clarity increases opportunity.

Communities benefit when members possess portable skills as well. Individuals who can adapt to changing conditions contribute to resilience within their networks. They can teach others, create businesses, and support collective progress when industries evolve.

Adaptability strengthens communities.

Ultimately, portable skills transform uncertainty into opportunity. Instead of fearing change, individuals with adaptable abilities can approach new environments with confidence. They know that their knowledge can be applied creatively to solve problems wherever they go.

Because the most powerful skill is not one that works in only one place.

It is one that works anywhere.

Principle of Law 29

Develop abilities that remain valuable across changing environments.

Portable skills protect independence.

Strategic Training Drill, Law 29

Strengthen your skill portability:

Identify abilities that apply across multiple industries.

Invest time in learning communication, leadership, and analytical thinking.

Continue updating your knowledge as technologies evolve.

Document projects and achievements that demonstrate your capabilities.

Ask yourself regularly:

Would my skills remain valuable if my current environment disappeared?

Portable skills transform change into opportunity.

Chapter Thirty

Chapter 30 Align Your Money With Your Mission

Money is directional power.

Every financial decision supports something. Whether through purchases, investments, donations, or savings, money flows toward activities that expand, survive, or decline depending on where resources are directed.

Spending and investing therefore function as choices about the future.

Resources shape outcomes.

Many individuals earn money without thinking carefully about how it is used beyond immediate needs. They work hard to generate income but spend it in ways that do not support their long-term goals. Over time, this disconnect creates a gap between what they believe in and what their financial habits actually reinforce.

Unaligned spending weakens purpose.

Strategic individuals approach money differently. They recognize that financial resources represent stored effort and opportunity. Because of this, they think carefully about how their money supports their broader mission in life.

Money becomes a tool for direction.

Mission refers to the deeper purpose guiding someone's decisions. For some individuals, this mission may involve building businesses, supporting family stability, contributing to community development, advancing knowledge, or pursuing creative work. When financial choices reflect these priorities, resources reinforce the path the individual intends to follow.

Purpose directs investment.

One example of alignment is education. Individuals who invest in learning, training, or skill development strengthen their ability to pursue meaningful work. Another example is entrepreneurship, where resources are directed toward creating businesses or projects that reflect personal vision and values.

Investment strengthens opportunity.

Another form of alignment involves supporting organizations, products, or initiatives that reflect one's principles. Financial support helps these initiatives grow and expand their influence. Over time, collective financial decisions can shape entire industries or social movements.

Money amplifies values.

Savings and investment also play a role in alignment. When individuals set aside resources for future opportunities, they create the ability to act when meaningful possibilities appear. This preparation transforms money from short-term consumption into long-term capability.

Preparation enables action.

Misalignment often occurs when financial habits follow impulse rather than intention. Advertising, social pressure, and short-term gratification can encourage spending patterns that do not support long-term objectives. Strategic individuals recognize these influences and maintain discipline in how they allocate resources.

Discipline preserves direction.

Another advantage of aligning money with mission is psychological clarity. When financial choices reflect personal values, individuals often experience greater satisfaction and motivation. Their work and spending feel connected to a meaningful purpose rather than disconnected obligations.

Alignment strengthens motivation.

Communities also benefit when members align their financial behavior with shared goals. Investments in education, businesses, and community projects can strengthen local economies and create opportunities for others. Collective financial alignment can therefore influence the growth and resilience of entire communities.

Shared investment builds progress.

Ultimately, the way money is used determines the kind of future that becomes possible. Resources directed toward meaningful goals gradually transform ideas into reality. Without intentional direction, those resources may instead strengthen systems that do not reflect one's values or aspirations.

Money builds what it feeds.

Strategic individuals therefore treat financial decisions as expressions of purpose. They evaluate whether each major financial choice contributes to the life they intend to build.

Because income alone does not determine influence.

What matters is how that income is directed.

Principle of Law 30

Direct your financial resources toward the goals and values you believe in.

Money becomes powerful when it supports your mission.

Strategic Training Drill, Law 30

Strengthen financial alignment:

Define the mission that guides your long-term decisions.

Evaluate whether your spending reflects that mission.

Invest in opportunities that expand your skills or impact.

Limit spending that distracts from long-term goals.

Ask yourself regularly:

What future am I building with the way I use my money?

Financial direction shapes the path ahead.

Chapter Thirty-One

Chapter 31 Keep Receipts, Records, and Redundancies

Documentation protects truth.

In every professional, legal, and economic environment, decisions are often evaluated through evidence rather than memory. People forget details, misunderstand conversations, or interpret events differently over time. When disagreements arise, the individual who possesses clear records often holds the strongest position.

Records create clarity.

Keeping receipts does not only refer to financial transactions. It includes written communication, agreements, contracts, project notes, performance reviews, timelines, and any documentation that demonstrates what occurred in a particular situation.

Evidence strengthens credibility.

In many institutions, disputes arise not because individuals intentionally misrepresent events, but because recollections differ. Without written documentation, resolving these disagreements becomes difficult. Records provide objective reference points that reduce confusion and clarify responsibilities.

Written history prevents uncertainty.

Another important advantage of documentation is accountability. When agreements are recorded clearly, expectations become visible to all participants. This visibility encourages responsible behavior because commitments are documented rather than assumed.

Clarity encourages integrity.

Financial documentation also protects economic stability. Receipts, invoices, tax records, and expense tracking allow individuals and businesses to monitor their financial activity accurately. Without organized records, errors can accumulate and create unnecessary complications.

Organization strengthens control.

Strategic individuals therefore develop systems for managing documentation effectively. Digital storage, labeled folders, backups, and organized files ensure that important information can be retrieved quickly when needed. These systems reduce stress and increase efficiency during critical situations.

Organization saves time.

Redundancy adds an additional layer of protection. Redundancy means maintaining copies of important information in more than one location. Digital files may be backed up to secure storage. Physical documents may be scanned and stored electronically. This approach prevents loss if one system fails.

Backup preserves security.

Redundancy also applies beyond documentation. Strategic individuals avoid relying entirely on single points of failure in their economic systems. Multiple communication channels, diversified investments, and alternative plans ensure that unexpected disruptions do not eliminate important resources.

Multiple layers create resilience.

Another benefit of records is long-term reflection. Documenting projects, decisions, and results allows individuals to review past experiences and learn from them. Patterns of success and mistakes become easier to identify when information has been recorded carefully.

History becomes instruction.

In professional environments, documentation also protects reputation. When individuals keep records of their contributions, achievements, and responsibilities, they can demonstrate the value they bring to an organization or project. This evidence supports fair recognition and career advancement.

Documentation defends contributions.

However, documentation should not be viewed as suspicion toward others. Instead, it represents responsible stewardship of information. Clear records help everyone involved understand expectations, decisions, and outcomes more effectively.

Transparency benefits everyone.

Over time, individuals who practice careful documentation gain a reputation for professionalism and reliability. Their organized approach to information allows them to respond confidently when questions arise. Others begin to trust their ability to manage complex responsibilities with precision.

Precision builds trust.

Ultimately, documentation transforms uncertainty into clarity. In environments where information may become confused or forgotten, records provide stable reference points that preserve truth and accountability.

Because in moments of disagreement, the strongest memory is not the loudest voice.

It is the documented fact.

Principle of Law 31

Protect your work and agreements through careful documentation.

Records create clarity, credibility, and protection.

Strategic Training Drill, Law 31

Strengthen your documentation discipline:

Keep organized records of important financial and professional activities.

Store critical documents in secure and accessible systems.

Maintain digital backups for important files.

Document agreements and commitments in writing whenever possible.

Ask yourself regularly:

If this situation were questioned later, would I have clear evidence?

Documentation preserves truth when memory fails.

Chapter Thirty-Two

PART V COLLECTIVE WARFARE: POWER AS A PEOPLE

PART V COLLECTIVE WARFARE: POWER AS A PEOPLE

LAW 32 Define Your People or Someone Else Will

Identity, Community, and Strategic Unity

The previous section focused on individual economic strength, ownership, insulation, skill mobility, and financial direction.

This section expands the conversation to something larger:

collective identity and collective power.

Throughout history, groups that clearly defined who they were and what they stood for were better able to protect their interests, organize their resources, and influence political and economic systems.

The first law of this section begins with identity itself.

LAW 32

Define Your People or Someone Else Will

Identity shapes power.

Every society organizes itself through categories and definitions. These definitions determine how groups are recognized legally, politically, and socially. They influence how resources are distributed, how rights are recognized, and how communities organize themselves.

When a group defines itself clearly, it gains the ability to shape its own narrative.

Self-definition creates direction.

When identity is unclear or externally imposed, others often fill the gap. Governments, institutions, media, or outside observers may assign labels that simplify or misunderstand the group's history and interests. These labels can influence how the group is perceived and how it is treated within broader systems.

External definitions shape perception.

Throughout history, many communities have struggled over the right to define their own identity. Cultural traditions, language, history, and shared experiences often form the foundation of these identities. When communities articulate these elements clearly, they create a stronger sense of shared purpose.

Shared identity strengthens cohesion.

Identity also plays a role in legal and political recognition. Many legal frameworks recognize communities based on clearly defined categories. These definitions may influence access to representation, protections, or opportunities within institutional systems.

Clarity strengthens recognition.

However, defining identity requires careful thought. Communities often contain diverse experiences, perspectives, and traditions. Effective identity frameworks therefore emphasize shared principles while respecting internal diversity.

Unity does not require uniformity.

Another advantage of self-definition is narrative control. When communities tell their own stories, they preserve their history and values accurately. This narrative provides guidance for future generations and prevents misunderstanding from replacing authentic memory.

Narrative preserves heritage.

Education plays an essential role in this process. When younger generations understand the history, achievements, and challenges of their community, they gain a stronger sense of belonging and responsibility. Education transforms identity from an abstract idea into a living tradition.

Knowledge sustains identity.

Self-definition also influences collective action. Communities with clear identities often organize more effectively around shared goals. They can advocate for policies, build institutions, and support economic development with greater coordination.

Clarity enables cooperation.

However, identity must remain adaptable. As societies evolve and new generations contribute their perspectives, communities often reinterpret their traditions in ways that remain relevant to contemporary challenges. This adaptability allows identity to remain meaningful rather than rigid.

Adaptability sustains continuity.

Strategic communities therefore approach identity as both inheritance and responsibility. They honor the experiences that shaped their past while also defining the principles that will guide their future.

Identity becomes both memory and direction.

Ultimately, defining identity is not merely a symbolic exercise. It shapes how communities understand themselves, how they organize collectively, and how they engage with the broader world.

Because if a people do not define themselves clearly...

Others will define them for their own purposes.

Principle of Law 32

Self-definition creates collective clarity.

Communities that define their identity intentionally can shape their own future.

Strategic Training Drill, Law 32

Strengthen collective identity awareness:

Study the history and traditions of your community.

Participate in conversations about shared values and goals.

Support institutions that preserve cultural knowledge.

Encourage education that teaches future generations about their heritage.

Ask yourself regularly:

How does my work contribute to the long-term strength of my community?

Identity becomes powerful when it guides collective purpose.

Chapter Thirty-Three

Chapter 33 Build Parallel Systems Quietly

Systems shape outcomes.

Throughout history, communities that desired long-term stability understood that influence does not come from protest alone. It comes from institutions, systems that provide education, economic opportunity, dispute resolution, and social support.

Institutions turn ideas into reality.

When communities rely entirely on systems built by others, their priorities may not always be reflected. External institutions often operate according to their own incentives, values, and historical development. As a result, the needs of specific communities may sometimes remain secondary within larger structures.

Dependence limits autonomy.

Parallel systems offer another approach.

A parallel system is not necessarily a replacement for existing institutions. Instead, it is a complementary structure built by a community to serve its own needs more directly. These systems operate alongside broader society while strengthening internal stability.

Parallel structures create resilience.

Examples of parallel systems throughout history include community schools, cooperative businesses, mutual aid networks, professional associations, cultural organizations, and community-based media. Each of these institutions allows people to collaborate around shared goals and provide services tailored to their community's needs.

Organization produces capability.

Parallel systems also promote leadership development. When communities build their own institutions, members gain opportunities to practice management, governance, entrepreneurship, and problem-solving. These experiences strengthen the collective skill base of the community.

Leadership grows through responsibility.

Another advantage of parallel systems is cultural preservation. Educational institutions, cultural centers, and media platforms allow communities to tell their own stories and maintain traditions that might otherwise fade within broader cultural currents.

Culture survives through institutions.

Economic systems are particularly important. Cooperative businesses, investment networks, and community development initiatives can circulate resources within the community and create opportunities for members to support one another economically.

Economic circulation builds stability.

However, effective parallel systems require patience and discipline. Building institutions takes time. It involves planning, governance structures, financial sustainability, and leadership continuity. Successful systems grow gradually through consistent effort.

Slow growth creates strong foundations.

Quiet construction can also be strategic. Rather than focusing solely on public visibility, many effective institutions begin with careful internal organization. Strong governance, clear missions, and reliable operations ensure that the institution can withstand challenges as it grows.

Strength precedes recognition.

Parallel systems also encourage collaboration across generations. Elders contribute wisdom and experience. Younger members bring innovation and energy. When these perspectives combine, institutions gain both continuity and adaptability.

Intergenerational cooperation strengthens longevity.

Importantly, parallel systems are not designed to isolate communities from society. Instead, they empower communities to participate in society from a position of greater strength and self-confidence.

Strength improves engagement.

Communities that develop their own institutions often become valuable contributors to broader society. Their organizations provide services, ideas, and innovations that enrich the larger social environment.

Empowered communities benefit everyone.

Ultimately, parallel systems transform aspiration into infrastructure. They create the educational, economic, and cultural foundations necessary for long-term growth.

Because while influence may begin with words...

It is sustained through institutions.

Principle of Law 33

Strong communities build institutions that reflect their values.

Parallel systems create stability, opportunity, and cultural continuity.

Strategic Training Drill, Law 33

Strengthen institutional thinking:

Identify community needs that existing institutions do not fully address.

Support organizations that serve those needs effectively.

Encourage leadership training within community institutions.

Invest time or resources into cooperative initiatives.

Ask yourself regularly:

What institutions must exist today to strengthen our community tomorrow?

Institutions transform vision into lasting impact.

Chapter Thirty-Four

Chapter 34 Invest in Community Identity, Not Popularity

Popularity is temporary.

Identity is permanent.

In modern society, attention often appears to be power. Social media metrics, public applause, and trending recognition can create the illusion that popularity equals influence. However, popularity is volatile. What is admired today can be forgotten tomorrow.

Attention moves quickly.

Communities that base their direction on popularity often find themselves chasing trends instead of building long-term stability.

Trends shift constantly, and decisions made to satisfy momentary approval may weaken deeper cultural foundations.

Trends do not build civilizations.

Identity operates differently. Identity is rooted in shared history, values, responsibilities, and purpose. When communities invest in strengthening their identity, they create a stable foundation that guides decisions across generations.

Identity creates continuity.

Many influential communities throughout history invested heavily in preserving language, traditions, institutions, and cultural memory. These investments allowed them to maintain coherence even during periods of political, economic, or social pressure.

Cultural memory sustains endurance.

Identity-based investment also shapes priorities. When a community understands who it is and what it stands for, it can evaluate opportunities more carefully. Decisions are measured against long-term values rather than short-term applause.

Purpose filters choices.

Popularity-driven behavior can also create internal division. When individuals compete primarily for recognition, rivalry may overshadow cooperation. In contrast, identity-centered communities emphasize shared responsibility and mutual progress.

Shared identity encourages unity.

Another advantage of identity investment is resilience. Communities grounded in strong identity often recover more effectively from external challenges because their members remain connected through common values and goals.

Identity strengthens resilience.

Education plays a central role in this process. Teaching younger generations about their cultural history, achievements, and responsibilities ensures that identity remains active rather than symbolic. Education turns heritage into practical guidance.

Knowledge preserves continuity.

Identity investment also influences economic and institutional development. When people support businesses, organizations, and initiatives that reflect their community's values, they strengthen the ecosystem that sustains collective progress.

Support builds infrastructure.

However, investing in identity does not require rejecting broader society. Communities can participate actively in wider social environments while maintaining a strong sense of who they are internally.

Participation and identity can coexist.

Strategic communities therefore focus less on external applause and more on internal alignment. Their primary goal is not to be admired by everyone, but to remain true to their principles and responsibilities.

Alignment builds strength.

Over time, communities grounded in identity often gain respect precisely because of their consistency. Others recognize that their actions reflect clear values rather than shifting trends.

Consistency creates credibility.

Ultimately, popularity may generate attention, but identity generates direction.

And direction is what sustains communities across generations.

Principle of Law 34

Popularity fades.

Identity endures.

Communities that invest in their identity build lasting influence.

Strategic Training Drill, Law 34

Strengthen identity-based decision making:

Study the core values that define your community.

Support institutions that preserve culture and knowledge.

Encourage younger generations to learn community history.

Evaluate opportunities based on long-term principles rather than immediate approval.

Ask yourself regularly:

Does this decision strengthen our identity or merely seek attention?

Identity transforms popularity into purpose.

Chapter Thirty-Five

Chapter 35 Empower Women as Core Builders of Nations

Civilizations begin in the home.

Every nation, community, and culture ultimately depends on the transmission of values, discipline, identity, and knowledge from one generation to the next. While institutions, governments, and economies play important roles, the earliest foundations of character and identity are formed within families and communities.

The first teachers are often mothers.

Across many cultures throughout history, women have served as central figures in preserving traditions, raising children, transmitting language, and shaping the moral structure of society. These roles influence not only individual development but also the long-term health of entire communities.

Nations are built through generations.

When women are respected, supported, and empowered within a community, the effects ripple outward. Children benefit from stronger guidance. Families gain stability. Communities develop deeper cultural continuity.

Stability strengthens societies.

Conversely, when women are marginalized or unsupported, the consequences can affect multiple generations. Families may struggle to maintain consistent guidance, and cultural traditions may weaken over time. The health of a community therefore depends on the well-being of those who nurture its future.

Support strengthens continuity.

Empowerment does not mean uniform roles or expectations. Women contribute to communities in many different ways — through leadership, education, entrepreneurship, public service, science, art, and countless other fields. The key principle is ensuring that women have the opportunity to develop their talents and contribute meaningfully to the collective good.

Opportunity expands contribution.

Education is especially important in this process. When women have access to education and professional development, their knowledge and skills enrich families, institutions, and economic systems. Education multiplies the capacity of a community to solve complex problems.

Knowledge multiplies influence.

Healthy societies also recognize the importance of partnership. Families and communities function best when men and women collaborate respectfully, combining their strengths to support shared goals. Mutual respect strengthens cooperation.

Partnership strengthens progress.

In addition to nurturing future generations, women often serve as powerful cultural anchors. They help maintain traditions, languages, stories, and ethical frameworks that define a community's identity. Their influence shapes how children understand who they are and where they come from.

Cultural memory preserves identity.

Empowering women therefore strengthens both present and future generations simultaneously. When women are supported in their roles as educators, leaders, and innovators, communities gain a deeper reservoir of wisdom, creativity, and resilience.

Strength expands capacity.

Another important dimension is leadership. Women throughout history have led movements, guided communities through crises, and contributed to intellectual and social progress. Their leadership broadens perspectives and strengthens decision-making processes.

Leadership diversifies insight.

Strategic communities therefore create environments where women can participate fully in civic life, economic development, and cultural preservation. They recognize that the success of future generations depends on the strength and stability of those who guide them.

Strong foundations produce strong nations.

Ultimately, empowering women is not merely an act of fairness, it is a strategic investment in the long-term vitality of a people.

Because the future of any nation is shaped by those who raise its children.

And those children become the builders of tomorrow's world.

Principle of Law 35

Empowering women strengthens families, communities, and future generations.

Healthy societies support those who nurture their future.

Strategic Training Drill, Law 35

Strengthen support for women's contributions:

Encourage educational opportunities for women and girls.

Recognize the leadership roles women play within communities.

Support institutions that promote family stability and mentorship.

Encourage collaboration between men and women in community initiatives.

Ask yourself regularly:

How can we strengthen the environment in which future generations are raised?

Strong foundations produce enduring societies.

Chapter Thirty-Six

Chapter 36 Train the Young in Duty and Purpose

Children inherit the future.

Every generation receives a society shaped by those who came before it. The ideas, institutions, and values that young people encounter during their formative years influence how they will lead, work, and contribute as adults.

Early guidance shapes destiny.

When children are raised with a clear sense of purpose, they often develop stronger discipline, confidence, and direction. Purpose provides a framework for understanding responsibility and encourages individuals to pursue goals that benefit both themselves and their communities.

Purpose builds character.

Many societies throughout history placed great emphasis on educating the young not only academically, but also morally and socially. Young people were taught the responsibilities associated with adulthood, leadership, and citizenship. These lessons helped prepare them to maintain and improve the institutions they would one day inherit.

Preparation builds continuity.

Training youth in duty does not require rigid instruction. Instead, it involves helping young people understand that their actions contribute to something larger than themselves. When youth recognize that they are part of a broader community, they often develop a deeper commitment to contributing positively.

Responsibility inspires growth.

Mentorship plays an essential role in this process. When experienced individuals take time to guide younger generations, they pass down valuable knowledge, practical skills, and wisdom learned from experience. Mentorship bridges the gap between generations.

Experience guides development.

Education also extends beyond formal schooling. Community organizations, cultural institutions, and family traditions all contribute to shaping how young people understand their role in society. These environments provide opportunities for youth to learn leadership, teamwork, and service.

Learning occurs everywhere.

Another important element of youth training is exposure to meaningful work. When young people participate in projects that require effort, collaboration, and accountability, they begin to understand the connection between discipline and achievement.

Work teaches responsibility.

Purposeful training also protects youth from confusion and discouragement. In a world filled with competing messages and distractions, clear guidance helps young people maintain focus on constructive paths that support their long-term success.

Clarity strengthens resilience.

Communities that invest in youth development often experience stronger long-term stability. Young people who feel valued and prepared are more likely to contribute their energy and creativity to building institutions, businesses, and cultural initiatives that strengthen society.

Prepared youth become capable adults.

However, training youth in duty should also encourage curiosity and innovation. While traditions provide valuable guidance, each generation must adapt to new circumstances. Encouraging young people to think critically allows them to build upon the wisdom of the past while addressing the challenges of the future.

Innovation ensures progress.

Balanced guidance therefore combines discipline with encouragement. Youth are taught responsibility while also being given opportunities to explore their talents and ideas. This balance allows them to develop both confidence and competence.

Confidence encourages leadership.

Ultimately, the strength of a community depends on the preparation of its next generation. When young people understand their responsibilities and believe their efforts matter, they develop the motivation to build a better future.

Because the future does not appear suddenly.

It is prepared by those who train the young to carry it forward.

Principle of Law 36

Nations endure when their youth are prepared with purpose, discipline, and responsibility.

The next generation must be trained to inherit the future.

Strategic Training Drill, Law 36

Strengthen youth development in your community:

Encourage mentorship relationships between experienced individuals and young people.

Support educational programs that teach leadership and responsibility.

Involve youth in meaningful community projects.

Teach the value of discipline, integrity, and service.

Ask yourself regularly:

How am I contributing to the preparation of the next generation?

Preparing the young strengthens the future.

Chapter Thirty-Seven

Chapter 37 Use History as a Weapon, Not a Crutch

History reveals patterns.

Every society is shaped by the events, struggles, achievements, and lessons of those who came before it. The study of history allows individuals and communities to understand how systems developed, how decisions were made, and how power shifted across time.

Patterns repeat.

When people study history carefully, they begin to notice recurring cycles in politics, economics, culture, and social movements. Recognizing these patterns helps individuals anticipate challenges and avoid repeating costly mistakes.

Knowledge prevents repetition.

However, history can be approached in two very different ways. Some individuals treat history primarily as a record of grievances. While understanding past injustices is important, dwelling exclusively on past harm can create a sense of helplessness that prevents forward progress.

Memory must inspire action.

A more strategic approach views history as a source of instruction. By analyzing both successes and failures from the past, individuals gain insight into what strategies worked, what obstacles appeared, and how communities overcame adversity.

History becomes guidance.

Communities that treat history as a weapon use it to inform their decisions. They examine how institutions were formed, how alliances were built, and how social movements achieved change. This knowledge strengthens strategic thinking.

Lessons strengthen strategy.

Historical awareness also deepens cultural identity. When people learn about the achievements, innovations, and resilience of their ancestors, they gain confidence in their ability to face present challenges. The past becomes a source of inspiration.

Pride strengthens perseverance.

Another advantage of studying history is recognizing how narratives shape perception. Different groups often interpret the same events in different ways. By examining multiple perspectives and primary sources, individuals develop a more nuanced understanding of historical events.

Critical thinking sharpens awareness.

History also provides warnings. Many societies have experienced similar challenges, including economic instability, political conflict, and cultural transformation. Understanding how previous generations responded to these circumstances helps communities prepare for future uncertainties.

Warnings protect the future.

Education plays a central role in preserving historical knowledge. Schools, cultural institutions, and community organizations help ensure that important stories, traditions, and lessons are not forgotten. When history is actively taught, it remains a living resource.

Education preserves memory.

However, historical knowledge must always be connected to present action. Studying the past without applying its lessons limits its value. The most powerful use of history occurs when individuals translate historical insight into modern strategies.

Application creates impact.

Communities that integrate historical awareness into their decision-making processes often develop stronger leadership, clearer identity, and more effective planning. They understand not only where they came from, but also where they want to go.

Direction emerges from understanding.

Ultimately, history should strengthen resolve rather than limit possibility. It should remind people of their capacity to overcome challenges and encourage them to build upon the achievements of those who came before them.

Because history is not meant to imprison the present.

It is meant to equip it.

Principle of Law 37

Study history for instruction, not limitation.

The past becomes powerful when its lessons guide the future.

Strategic Training Drill, Law 37

Strengthen historical awareness:

Study the major events that shaped your community and society.

Examine both achievements and mistakes from past generations.

Seek multiple perspectives when studying historical events.

Apply historical lessons to modern decisions and strategies.

Ask yourself regularly:

What lessons from the past can help guide today's challenges?

History becomes powerful when it informs action.

Chapter Thirty-Eight

Chapter 38 Separate Emotion From Strategy

Emotion is natural.

Strategy is intentional.

Human beings experience powerful emotions, anger, frustration, fear, pride, and excitement. These emotions often arise when people care deeply about a situation or believe something important is at stake.

Emotion signals importance.

However, effective decision-making requires more than emotional reaction. Strategic thinking involves analyzing situations carefully, considering possible outcomes, and choosing actions that align with long-term goals rather than momentary impulses.

Strategy requires patience.

Many conflicts escalate when individuals react emotionally instead of strategically. In heated moments, words and actions may be chosen quickly without fully considering their consequences. These reactions can complicate situations and create obstacles that might otherwise have been avoided.

Impulse often creates difficulty.

Strategic individuals therefore develop the ability to pause before responding. This pause allows them to evaluate the situation objectively and choose responses that support their broader goals.

Pause creates clarity.

Separating emotion from strategy does not mean ignoring feelings. Emotions can provide valuable information about what matters to us and what we believe is right. The key is ensuring that emotions inform our understanding without controlling our decisions.

Emotion informs awareness.

Strategic thinking also requires perspective. When individuals step back from a situation and consider multiple viewpoints, they gain a clearer understanding of the factors involved. This broader perspective helps them identify solutions that might not be visible during emotional reactions.

Perspective strengthens judgment.

Another advantage of emotional discipline is credibility. People who remain calm and composed during difficult situations often earn the trust and respect of others. Their steady approach signals reliability and thoughtful leadership.

Calm builds confidence.

In professional and organizational environments, emotional control can prevent misunderstandings and unnecessary conflict. Clear communication and measured responses allow problems to be addressed constructively rather than escalating into personal disputes.

Composure supports cooperation.

Communities also benefit when leaders practice emotional discipline. Leaders who analyze situations carefully before acting are more likely to guide their communities through challenges with wisdom and stability.

Leadership requires balance.

Developing this skill requires practice. Techniques such as reflection, active listening, and careful communication help individuals strengthen their ability to think strategically even in stressful situations.

Practice strengthens discipline.

Over time, individuals who cultivate this balance between awareness and restraint become more effective decision-makers. They recognize emotional signals while ensuring that their actions reflect thoughtful planning.

Balance strengthens effectiveness.

Ultimately, separating emotion from strategy allows individuals and communities to act with clarity rather than impulse.

Because powerful emotions may start movements.

But thoughtful strategy sustains them.

Principle of Law 38

Emotion reveals what matters.

Strategy determines how to act.

Wise decisions balance both.

Strategic Training Drill, Law 38

Strengthen emotional discipline.

Pause before responding during tense situations.

Ask yourself what outcome you truly want from the situation.

Consider multiple perspectives before making decisions.

Practice calm communication when disagreements arise.

Ask yourself regularly:

Am I reacting emotionally, or responding strategically?

Clarity turns emotion into effective action.

Chapter Thirty-Nine

Chapter 39 Fight for Human Rights, Not Civil Rights

The language of rights determines the arena of struggle.

Throughout modern history, many movements have advocated for equality and justice through the framework of civil rights. Civil rights generally refer to protections and freedoms granted within a specific nation's legal system. They address how citizens are treated under the laws and institutions of that country.

Civil rights operate within a national framework.

Because civil rights are defined by domestic law, they are typically interpreted and enforced through the courts, legislatures, and political systems of the nation in which they exist. Advocates working within this framework often seek policy reforms, legal protections, and equal treatment under existing institutions.

Domestic law shapes civil rights.

Human rights, however, operate on a broader level. Human rights refer to fundamental rights believed to belong to all people simply by virtue of being human. These principles are reflected in international agreements and declarations developed by global organizations and treaties.

Human rights extend beyond national boundaries.

When issues are framed as human rights concerns, they may enter international conversations about dignity, equality, and justice. These frameworks can involve international institutions, global advocacy networks, and diplomatic dialogue.

Global principles expand the conversation.

The distinction between civil rights and human rights therefore influences strategy. Civil rights approaches often focus on reforming policies within a country's existing legal structure. Human rights approaches may emphasize universal principles that transcend any single national system.

Different frameworks create different avenues for action.

Understanding both frameworks can help communities navigate complex legal and political environments. Some issues may be addressed effectively through domestic policy reform, while others may benefit from broader international attention or collaboration.

Strategic awareness expands options.

Legal scholars, activists, and policymakers often study international conventions, human rights declarations, and constitutional law to understand how these frameworks interact. This knowledge allows advocates to choose approaches that best align with their goals and circumstances.

Knowledge strengthens advocacy.

Education plays a key role in this process. When individuals understand the legal language surrounding rights and protections, they become more capable of participating in civic dialogue and contributing to meaningful reform efforts.

Legal literacy empowers citizens.

Communities that understand both civil and human rights frameworks often gain greater flexibility in addressing challenges. They can engage in local advocacy while also participating in global conversations about justice and equality.

Multiple strategies strengthen influence.

However, effective advocacy requires careful preparation. Legal arguments, historical context, and well-documented evidence are essential components of persuasive rights-based approaches. Strategic planning helps ensure that advocacy efforts are both credible and constructive.

Preparation strengthens impact.

Ultimately, the language of rights shapes the path toward change. Understanding the difference between civil rights and human rights allows communities to engage thoughtfully with the legal systems that govern their societies while also recognizing broader principles of human dignity.

Because the way a struggle is defined...

Often determines the stage upon which it is fought.

Principle of Law 39

Understanding the frameworks of civil rights and human rights expands the range of possible strategies for justice and reform.

Knowledge of law strengthens effective advocacy.

Strategic Training Drill, Law 39

Strengthen legal awareness:

Study the basic principles of civil rights law within your country.

Learn about international human rights declarations and conventions.

Encourage civic education that promotes legal literacy.

Support organizations that advocate for justice through lawful means.

Ask yourself regularly:

What legal framework best supports the change we seek?

Understanding the language of rights expands strategic possibility.

Chapter Forty

PART VI THE ASCENSION: SUPREME POWER HABITS

PART VI THE ASCENSION: SUPREME POWER HABITS

LAW 40 Practice Strategic Minimalism

Long-Term Strategy, Personal Governance, and Sovereign Identity

The previous sections explored identity, systems, relationships, economics, and collective strategy.

This final section moves deeper into personal mastery and long-range thinking. It focuses on the habits that allow individuals and communities to sustain power across decades rather than moments.

The first law of this section introduces a principle often overlooked in modern society.

power grows through disciplined simplicity.

LAW 40

Practice Strategic Minimalism

Power often grows through reduction, not accumulation.

Modern culture frequently encourages people to pursue more, more possessions, more obligations, more commitments, and more distractions. While some expansion can be beneficial, constant accumulation can also dilute focus and energy.

Excess fragments attention.

Strategic minimalism takes a different approach. Instead of filling life with endless activity, it focuses on clarifying priorities and removing unnecessary complexity. By reducing distractions, individuals gain the ability to concentrate their energy on what truly matters.

Clarity strengthens focus.

Minimalism in this sense is not about deprivation. It is about intentional selection. Strategic individuals choose carefully which commitments, relationships, and activities deserve their time and effort.

Intentional choices create direction.

When life becomes overloaded with competing demands, even talented individuals struggle to make meaningful progress. Energy becomes scattered across too many objectives, leaving little strength available for the goals that matter most.

Scattered effort weakens results.

Strategic minimalism therefore begins with identifying core priorities. These priorities may include personal growth, family, education, economic stability, community involvement, or creative pursuits. Once priorities are clear, unnecessary distractions can be reduced.

Priorities guide discipline.

Another benefit of minimalism is improved decision-making. When individuals maintain fewer obligations, they have greater mental space to evaluate opportunities thoughtfully. This clarity allows them to choose projects and partnerships that align with their long-term goals.

Mental space strengthens judgment.

Minimalism also protects personal energy. Every commitment requires time, attention, and emotional investment. By limiting commitments to those that truly matter, individuals preserve the energy needed to perform their responsibilities effectively.

Energy becomes concentrated.

This principle applies to organizations and communities as well. Institutions that focus on a clear mission often outperform those attempting to pursue too many goals simultaneously. Strategic focus allows resources to be used more effectively.

Focus strengthens institutions.

Another aspect of strategic minimalism involves information management. In a world saturated with constant news, social media updates, and digital communication, individuals must decide which information deserves their attention.

Attention is a valuable resource.

Choosing carefully what to read, watch, and engage with prevents unnecessary mental clutter. This allows individuals to dedicate more time to learning, planning, and creating meaningful work.

Disciplined attention builds insight.

Strategic minimalism also encourages patience. When people are not rushing from one distraction to another, they gain the opportunity to reflect deeply on their goals and values. Reflection often reveals opportunities that might otherwise remain hidden.

Stillness reveals clarity.

Over time, individuals who practice strategic minimalism develop a reputation for focus and reliability. Others recognize that their decisions are guided by careful thought rather than impulsive reaction.

Consistency builds credibility.

Ultimately, the purpose of strategic minimalism is not to shrink life, but to strengthen it. By removing unnecessary complexity, individuals create space for the pursuits that truly shape their destiny.

Because power rarely grows through chaos.

It grows through clarity, discipline, and focus.

Principle of Law 40

Reduce distractions so that energy can be directed toward meaningful goals.

Clarity strengthens power.

Strategic Training Drill, Law 40

Practice strategic minimalism:

Identify the three most important priorities in your life.

Reduce commitments that do not support those priorities.

Limit exposure to distractions that consume attention without adding value.

Schedule time for reflection and planning.

Ask yourself regularly:

Is this activity strengthening my purpose or diluting it?

Focused effort multiplies impact.

Chapter Forty-One

Chapter 41 Build a System, Not a Lifestyle

Lifestyles depend on motivation.

Systems depend on structure.

Many people attempt to achieve their goals through bursts of motivation. They become inspired, work intensely for a short period, and then gradually lose momentum as daily distractions return. When motivation fades, progress often stalls.

Motivation is temporary.

Systems operate differently. A system is a structured process designed to produce consistent outcomes regardless of mood or momentary enthusiasm. Systems transform goals from occasional efforts into regular habits.

Structure creates consistency.

For example, someone who wants to improve their health may rely on motivation to exercise occasionally. But someone who builds a system schedules regular exercise, tracks progress, and creates routines that make healthy behavior easier to maintain.

Routine sustains progress.

The same principle applies to education, career development, financial management, and creative work. Individuals who rely on motivation alone often struggle with inconsistency. Those who design systems create environments that encourage steady improvement.

Consistency compounds results.

Systems also reduce decision fatigue. When routines and processes are already established, individuals spend less time deciding what to do next. Instead, they simply follow the structure they have created.

Automation strengthens discipline.

Organizations operate according to this principle as well. Businesses, institutions, and governments function through systems, procedures, policies, and processes that guide daily operations. These systems allow complex organizations to operate efficiently.

Systems scale influence.

Another advantage of systems is resilience. Motivation may fluctuate during difficult times, but well-designed systems continue functioning even during periods of stress or uncertainty.

Structure survives pressure.

Effective systems usually contain several key components: clear goals, defined processes, measurable progress indicators, and regular review. These elements ensure that the system remains aligned with its intended purpose.

Measurement enables improvement.

Systems also allow individuals to delegate responsibilities more effectively. When processes are clearly defined, others can participate without confusion. This allows projects and institutions to grow beyond the limitations of one person's time and energy.

Structure enables collaboration.

Importantly, systems should remain adaptable. As circumstances change, systems may need adjustment to remain effective. Regular evaluation ensures that processes continue serving their intended goals.

Adaptability strengthens longevity.

Over time, individuals who build strong systems often achieve greater stability and productivity than those who rely solely on bursts of effort. Their success is not dependent on mood, inspiration, or external pressure.

Their systems carry them forward.

Ultimately, the difference between a lifestyle and a system is durability. A lifestyle may reflect temporary habits or preferences. A system creates a framework that supports progress across years and decades.

Because motivation may begin a journey.

But systems ensure the journey continues.

Principle of Law 41

Design systems that support your goals consistently.

Structure transforms intention into lasting progress.

Strategic Training Drill, Law 41

Strengthen your personal systems:

Identify a goal that requires long-term effort.

Design a routine or process that supports steady progress toward that goal.

Track measurable indicators to evaluate progress.

Review and adjust your system regularly to improve effectiveness.

Ask yourself regularly:

Does my system make success easier or harder to achieve?

Systems turn discipline into momentum.

Chapter Forty-Two

Chapter 42 Avoid Internal Civil War

Internal conflict destroys more power than external opposition.

Throughout history, many movements, organizations, and communities have faced challenges from outside forces. Yet often the most damaging conflicts arise not from external pressure, but from divisions within the group itself.

Internal struggles weaken unity.

When individuals who share common goals begin fighting one another, energy that could have been directed toward building institutions or solving problems becomes consumed by rivalry, distrust, and competition.

Energy becomes misdirected.

Internal conflict can arise for many reasons: misunderstandings, personality differences, competition for recognition, or disagreements about strategy. While disagreement is natural in any group, unmanaged conflict can escalate into divisions that harm the entire community.

Disagreement becomes division.

Strategic individuals and communities therefore recognize the importance of maintaining unity even when differences exist. They understand that disagreement can be addressed through dialogue, patience, and structured decision-making processes.

Communication restores clarity.

Another cause of internal conflict is the struggle for personal recognition. When individuals prioritize status over shared goals, cooperation becomes more difficult. The focus shifts from collective progress to personal advantage.

Ego disrupts collaboration.

Healthy organizations encourage humility and mutual respect among their members. When individuals remember the broader mission that brought them together, they are more likely to resolve disagreements constructively.

Purpose strengthens unity.

Leadership plays a critical role in managing internal conflict. Leaders who encourage transparency, fair decision-making, and open communication can help prevent misunderstandings from escalating into larger disputes.

Fairness builds trust.

Another important strategy is establishing clear structures for resolving disagreements. Committees, mediation processes, and transparent policies allow concerns to be addressed without damaging relationships.

Structure prevents escalation.

Communities must also remember that diversity of thought can be beneficial. Different perspectives can improve decision-making when they are discussed respectfully. Constructive debate often leads to stronger ideas and more effective solutions.

Diversity strengthens insight.

However, debate must remain focused on solving problems rather than attacking individuals. When discussions become personal, collaboration breaks down and the group's ability to move forward is weakened.

Respect protects cooperation.

Strategic communities also remain aware that external challenges sometimes intensify internal tensions. Stress, uncertainty, and competition for resources can increase the likelihood of disagreement. Recognizing these pressures allows communities to address them thoughtfully.

Awareness reduces conflict.

Ultimately, unity does not require absolute agreement. It requires shared commitment to the greater purpose that brought individuals together in the first place.

Shared purpose sustains cooperation.

Communities that manage internal differences wisely preserve their energy for the work that truly matters: building institutions, strengthening relationships, and improving the future for those who will follow.

Because history shows that many great movements were not defeated from outside.

They were weakened from within.

Principle of Law 42

Protect unity by resolving disagreements constructively.

Internal cooperation preserves collective strength.

Strategic Training Drill, Law 42

Strengthen unity within your community or organization:

Address disagreements through respectful dialogue.

Focus discussions on solving problems rather than assigning blame.

Support leadership structures that encourage fairness and transparency.

Remember the shared purpose that unites participants.

Ask yourself regularly:

Is this conflict helping us grow, or distracting us from our mission?

Unity multiplies strength.

Chapter Forty-Three

Chapter 43 Think in 10-Year Vision Cycles

Most people plan for the week.

Strategic individuals plan for the decade.

Modern life often encourages short-term thinking. Many decisions revolve around immediate concerns, daily schedules, monthly expenses, or yearly goals. While short-term planning is necessary, relying exclusively on it can limit the scale of what individuals and communities achieve.

Short horizons shrink ambition.

Long-term thinkers approach life differently. They ask questions that extend beyond immediate circumstances: Where should my skills be in ten years? What institutions should exist ten years from now? What future am I helping to build?

Vision expands possibility.

Thinking in ten-year cycles allows individuals to make decisions with patience and clarity. Goals that seem overwhelming in the short term become manageable when viewed as part of a longer journey. Each year becomes a step toward a broader vision.

Time multiplies progress.

Another advantage of long-term thinking is strategic patience. Many meaningful achievements, building institutions, mastering skills, developing businesses, strengthening communities, require sustained effort over extended periods. Short-term expectations can cause people to abandon efforts before results appear.

Patience protects perseverance.

Ten-year thinking also encourages investment in education and skill development. Individuals who imagine their future capabilities often recognize the importance of learning today. Each skill acquired becomes a tool that supports future opportunities.

Learning compounds value.

Communities benefit from long-term planning as well. When organizations develop visions that extend beyond immediate challenges, they can coordinate projects that build infrastructure, leadership development, and economic growth across generations.

Planning strengthens institutions.

Another important aspect of long-term thinking is resilience. When individuals encounter setbacks, a decade-long vision reminds them that temporary obstacles do not define the entire journey. Difficult moments become lessons rather than final outcomes.

Perspective strengthens endurance.

Long-term thinking also encourages responsible decision-making. Actions taken today can affect opportunities years into the future. Considering these consequences helps individuals choose paths that align with their values and long-term objectives.

Foresight improves choices.

However, long-term vision should remain flexible. Circumstances change, and new information may require adjustments to the plan. Strategic individuals revisit their long-term goals periodically and refine their path accordingly.

Adaptation maintains relevance.

Another benefit of decade-level thinking is clarity of priorities. When individuals ask themselves what truly matters over the next ten years, many short-term distractions lose their importance. Time and energy are redirected toward meaningful work.

Clarity strengthens discipline.

Ultimately, thinking in ten-year cycles transforms the way individuals approach their lives. It replaces reaction with intention and replaces short-term urgency with thoughtful preparation.

Because great achievements rarely emerge from hurried decisions.

They grow from long vision, steady effort, and disciplined patience.

Principle of Law 43

Plan beyond the present moment.

Long-term vision turns small daily efforts into lasting accomplishments.

Strategic Training Drill, Law 43

Strengthen long-term vision:

Imagine where you want to be in ten years.

Identify the skills and knowledge required to reach that vision.

Break long-term goals into yearly milestones.

Review your progress regularly and adjust your plan when necessary.

Ask yourself regularly:

Is this decision helping or hindering my ten-year vision?

A decade of focused effort can transform a lifetime.

Chapter Forty-Four

Chapter 44 Master the Art of Dual Identity

Wisdom knows when to reveal and when to reserve.

Throughout life, individuals move through many environments, family spaces, professional environments, public institutions, social settings, and private circles. Each environment often operates with its own expectations, language, and behavioral norms.

Context shapes interaction.

Strategic individuals understand that navigating these environments effectively sometimes requires adjusting how they present themselves. They learn to communicate in ways that are appropriate for the setting while maintaining their core values internally.

Adaptation enables movement.

Dual identity does not mean dishonesty or abandoning one's principles. Instead, it reflects the ability to maintain a clear inner identity while demonstrating situational awareness in public environments.

Inner stability supports outer flexibility.

For example, professionals often speak differently in a workplace meeting than they would in a conversation with close friends or family members. This shift in tone and behavior is not deception, it is social awareness.

Awareness improves communication.

Strategic individuals recognize that public environments sometimes require diplomacy, restraint, and careful presentation. At the same time, private spaces allow for deeper expression of personal beliefs, cultural identity, and emotional honesty.

Different spaces allow different expressions.

Maintaining this balance helps individuals protect both their integrity and their effectiveness. When someone expresses every thought impulsively in every environment, misunderstandings can occur and opportunities may be lost.

Disciplined expression preserves opportunity.

Another advantage of mastering dual identity is psychological stability. When individuals know clearly who they are internally, external pressures have less power to shape their sense of self. They can navigate complex environments without feeling that they must abandon their identity.

Self-knowledge protects confidence.

Many successful leaders throughout history demonstrated this ability. They communicated differently depending on the audience while remaining guided by a consistent set of principles. Their adaptability allowed them to build alliances and solve problems across diverse environments.

Adaptability expands influence.

This skill is also valuable in multicultural and global environments where individuals interact with people from many different backgrounds. Understanding how to communicate respectfully across cultural contexts improves cooperation and mutual understanding.

Cultural awareness builds bridges.

However, mastering dual identity requires reflection and discipline. Individuals must define their core values clearly so that external adaptation does not lead to internal confusion. When core principles are well understood, adaptation becomes a tool rather than a compromise.

Clarity preserves authenticity.

Another important element is emotional intelligence. Recognizing the expectations and sensitivities of different environments allows individuals to choose the most constructive way to express their ideas.

Emotional intelligence improves strategy.

Over time, individuals who master this balance gain the ability to move effectively across many environments without losing their sense of purpose. Their adaptability allows them to build relationships, share ideas, and contribute meaningfully in a wide range of settings.

Flexibility strengthens influence.

Ultimately, mastering dual identity means understanding that identity has both private depth and public strategy.

One preserves the soul.

The other protects the mission.

Principle of Law 44

Maintain a strong inner identity while adapting wisely to different environments.

Self-knowledge allows flexibility without compromise.

Strategic Training Drill, Law 44

Strengthen situational awareness:

Define your core values clearly so they remain stable in every environment.

Observe how communication styles differ across settings.

Practice expressing ideas in ways appropriate for different audiences.

Maintain private spaces where your full identity can be expressed freely.

Ask yourself regularly:

Am I adapting strategically while remaining true to my principles?

Balance between authenticity and adaptability strengthens influence.

Chapter Forty-Five

Chapter 45 Conserve Energy for Battles That Matter

Energy is a limited resource.

Every day, individuals encounter situations that demand attention, disagreements, distractions, criticisms, minor conflicts, and competing priorities. If one attempts to engage every issue with equal intensity, exhaustion quickly follows.

Constant reaction drains strength.

Strategic individuals recognize that power is not measured by how many battles one fights, but by how wisely those battles are chosen. They understand that energy, time, and focus must be directed toward goals that truly matter.

Selection creates strength.

Many conflicts arise from misunderstandings, impulsive comments, or temporary frustrations. Engaging every minor dispute can consume valuable time without producing meaningful results. Strategic thinkers therefore learn to distinguish between momentary distractions and issues of genuine importance.

Discernment protects focus.

Choosing not to engage in every disagreement does not indicate weakness. In many cases, restraint demonstrates maturity and strategic awareness. By refusing to be drawn into unnecessary conflicts, individuals preserve their attention for challenges that require thoughtful effort.

Restraint strengthens control.

Another advantage of conserving energy is improved decision-making. When individuals avoid constant reaction, they gain time to reflect and evaluate situations carefully. This reflection allows them to identify the moments when decisive action is truly necessary.

Calm strengthens judgment.

Strategic patience also prevents emotional exhaustion. Continuous conflict can drain motivation and damage relationships. By reserving energy for meaningful work and constructive challenges, individuals maintain the endurance required for long-term progress.

Endurance sustains effort.

This principle applies not only to individuals but also to organizations and communities. Groups that become entangled in endless internal disputes often lose sight of their larger mission. Their resources are consumed by conflict rather than growth.

Conflict disrupts progress.

Strategic organizations therefore prioritize their objectives carefully. They focus on initiatives that advance their mission and avoid becoming distracted by issues that do not contribute to long-term goals.

Focus preserves direction.

Another aspect of conserving energy involves recognizing when to disengage temporarily. Sometimes stepping back from a situation allows emotions to settle and perspectives to broaden. When individuals return with clearer minds, they are better prepared to address the issue productively.

Distance restores clarity.

Over time, individuals who practice disciplined engagement develop a reputation for wisdom. Others recognize that when they do choose to act, their actions carry purpose and seriousness.

Selective action builds credibility.

Ultimately, conserving energy ensures that effort remains aligned with purpose. When individuals invest their strength in the challenges that truly matter, their work becomes more effective and sustainable.

Because not every hill must be climbed.

And not every argument must be won.

The true measure of strategy is knowing which battles shape the future.

Principle of Law 45

Direct your energy toward meaningful goals rather than momentary conflicts.

Wise restraint strengthens long-term influence.

Strategic Training Drill, Law 45

Strengthen strategic focus:

Before engaging in conflict, ask whether the issue truly affects your long-term goals.

Practice pausing before reacting to criticism or provocation.

Prioritize tasks that contribute directly to your mission.

Allow minor disagreements to pass when they do not require action.

Ask yourself regularly:

Is this battle worth the energy it demands?

Focused energy produces meaningful results.

Chapter Forty-Six

Chapter 46 Audit Your Circle Often

Your environment shapes your trajectory.

Human beings are deeply influenced by the people they spend time with. Friends, colleagues, mentors, and partners all contribute to the attitudes, expectations, and behaviors that gradually become part of everyday life.

Influence spreads quietly.

When individuals surround themselves with people who encourage growth, responsibility, and thoughtful decision-making, those values often become reinforced through daily interaction. Positive environments support constructive habits and healthy ambition.

Support strengthens progress.

Conversely, environments that normalize negativity, constant conflict, or lack of discipline can gradually undermine even the most determined individuals. Over time, repeated exposure to these influences can weaken motivation and cloud judgment.

Environment affects perspective.

Strategic individuals therefore review their social and professional circles periodically. This review is not an act of judgment against others; rather, it is a thoughtful evaluation of whether the relationships in one's life support personal growth and shared goals.

Reflection protects direction.

An effective circle often contains several types of relationships. Mentors offer wisdom and experience. Peers provide collaboration and encouragement. Younger individuals benefit from guidance and contribute fresh perspectives.

Balanced circles promote growth.

Trust is another important factor. Relationships built on honesty and mutual respect create environments where individuals feel safe sharing ideas, asking questions, and learning from mistakes.

Trust strengthens cooperation.

Strategic circles also encourage accountability. Friends and colleagues who offer constructive feedback help individuals recognize areas for improvement and maintain high standards in their work and behavior.

Accountability strengthens character.

Another benefit of auditing one's circle is recognizing when relationships have naturally changed over time. As individuals grow, their priorities and responsibilities may evolve. Periodic reflection allows people to maintain connections that remain supportive while respectfully adjusting those that no longer align with their direction.

Growth changes relationships.

This process should be approached with humility and empathy. Every individual is navigating their own journey, and relationships should be treated with care and respect. The goal is not exclusion but alignment.

Respect preserves dignity.

Communities and organizations also benefit from thoughtful relationship management. Teams that share common values and goals tend to collaborate more effectively, solve problems creatively, and maintain stability during challenges.

Alignment strengthens institutions.

Over time, individuals who cultivate supportive circles often experience greater personal and professional development. Their environment becomes a source of encouragement, knowledge, and opportunity.

Positive networks create momentum.

Ultimately, auditing one's circle is about ensuring that the relationships surrounding you contribute positively to the direction you wish to pursue.

Because the people closest to you often influence the paths you walk.

Choose wisely, and review often.

Principle of Law 46

Your environment influences your growth.

Surround yourself with people who support constructive progress.

Strategic Training Drill, Law 46

Strengthen your circle intentionally:

Reflect on the people who most influence your daily thinking and habits.

Seek mentors who demonstrate wisdom and integrity.

Maintain friendships that encourage mutual growth.

Offer support to others who are striving toward meaningful goals.

Ask yourself regularly:

Do the people around me strengthen the direction I want to go?

Strong circles support strong futures.

Chapter Forty-Seven

Chapter 47 Reinvent Yourself Without Losing Your Core

Growth requires change.

Throughout life, individuals encounter new experiences, responsibilities, and opportunities. As circumstances evolve, the skills, knowledge, and perspectives that once served a person well may need to be expanded or refined.

Adaptation supports progress.

Many people resist change because it feels uncomfortable or uncertain. Yet those who refuse to adapt risk becoming disconnected from the environments around them. Strategic individuals recognize that reinvention is a natural part of personal and professional development.

Evolution sustains relevance.

Reinvention does not mean abandoning one's identity or values. Instead, it involves building upon a stable foundation while developing new abilities that allow individuals to meet emerging challenges.

The core remains constant.

For example, a person who begins their career as a student eventually becomes a professional, mentor, or leader. Each stage requires different skills and perspectives. Reinvention allows individuals to grow into these new roles effectively.

Roles change over time.

Learning plays a central role in this process. Individuals who continue studying new ideas, technologies, and disciplines expand their capacity to contribute meaningfully in changing environments.

Learning fuels transformation.

Reinvention also requires humility. Accepting that one must grow beyond previous limitations encourages openness to feedback, mentorship, and experimentation. These experiences often reveal opportunities that were previously invisible.

Humility opens doors.

Another advantage of reinvention is resilience. When individuals possess multiple skills and perspectives, they are better prepared to adapt when circumstances change unexpectedly. Flexibility allows them to navigate transitions without losing momentum.

Flexibility protects stability.

Communities and organizations also benefit from this principle. Institutions that periodically reassess their strategies and adapt to new conditions often remain effective across generations. Those that resist change risk becoming outdated.

Adaptable institutions endure.

However, reinvention must remain anchored to a stable core. Values such as integrity, responsibility, and commitment provide continuity even as methods evolve. Without a clear core identity, change can become confusion rather than progress.

Values provide direction.

Strategic individuals therefore maintain a balance between stability and evolution. They protect their guiding principles while remaining open to learning new approaches and exploring new possibilities.

Balance creates wisdom.

Over time, individuals who practice thoughtful reinvention often become more versatile and capable. Their experiences across different roles and environments give them deeper insight into the complexities of life and leadership.

Experience deepens understanding.

Ultimately, reinvention ensures that growth continues throughout life. It allows individuals to respond creatively to change while preserving the values that define who they are.

Because the world never stands still.

And those who grow with it remain prepared for the future.

Principle of Law 47

Adapt your methods while preserving your core values.

Growth requires both stability and evolution.

Strategic Training Drill, Law 47

Strengthen your ability to evolve:

Identify areas where new skills could improve your effectiveness.

Continue learning through books, courses, and mentorship.

Reflect periodically on how your goals and roles are changing.

Experiment with new approaches while maintaining your core values.

Ask yourself regularly:

How must I grow to meet the opportunities of the future?

Reinvention keeps progress alive.

Chapter Forty-Eight

PART VII THE FINAL LAW

PART VII THE FINAL LAW

The Principle That Governs All Others

LAW 48

Self-Determination Is the Highest Form of Power

The greatest power any individual or people can possess is the authority to define themselves.

Throughout history, control has often been exercised not only through physical force or economic dominance but through the power to define identity, narrative, and possibility. When one group controls how another group is described, classified, or understood, it gains influence over how that group is treated within society.

Definitions shape reality.

Self-determination challenges this dynamic. It begins with the recognition that every individual and community possesses the right to define who they are, what they value, and the future they intend to build.

Identity begins internally.

When individuals accept definitions imposed upon them by external forces, their sense of possibility can become limited. Labels may shape expectations, influence opportunities, and affect how people perceive their own potential.

External definitions restrict freedom.

Self-determination reverses this process. It places the authority of identity back into the hands of the individual or community. Instead of accepting imposed narratives, people choose the values, goals, and principles that guide their lives.

Self-definition restores agency.

This principle extends beyond personal identity. Self-determination also influences economic independence, educational priorities, cultural preservation, and political participation. Communities that define their own direction often develop institutions that reflect their values and support their long-term goals.

Direction shapes development.

Another important dimension of self-determination is responsibility. When individuals claim the authority to define themselves, they also accept the responsibility to act with integrity, discipline, and foresight. True autonomy requires thoughtful stewardship of one's decisions and actions.

Freedom requires responsibility.

Self-determination therefore combines both liberty and accountability. It empowers individuals to pursue their goals while encouraging them to consider how their choices contribute to the well-being of the communities to which they belong.

Responsibility strengthens freedom.

Education and awareness play vital roles in this process. When individuals understand their history, their rights, and the systems within which they operate, they become better equipped to make informed decisions about their future.

Knowledge strengthens autonomy.

Communities that embrace self-determination often cultivate leadership, creativity, and resilience. Their members feel a stronger sense of ownership over their institutions and initiatives because they know that the direction of their community depends on their participation.

Participation builds strength.

Self-determination also encourages cooperation among individuals who share common goals. When people recognize their ability to shape their collective future, they often work together to build systems that support mutual progress.

Shared vision strengthens unity.

At the same time, self-determination respects diversity within communities. Individuals may pursue different paths while remaining connected by shared principles of dignity, responsibility, and mutual respect.

Freedom allows diversity.

Ultimately, self-determination represents the culmination of all the laws presented in this book. Identity, strategy, discipline, economic independence, community development, and long-term vision all contribute to the ability of individuals and communities to shape their own destiny.

All power flows toward autonomy.

Because the greatest victory is not merely overcoming obstacles imposed by others.

It is possessing the confidence and capability to determine your own path.

Principle of Law 48

Self-determination is the highest form of power.

The authority to define your identity, values, and direction shapes every other form of influence.

Strategic Training Drill, Law 48

Strengthen your practice of self-determination:

Define the values that guide your life and decisions.

Pursue education that deepens your understanding of the systems around you.

Participate in building institutions that reflect your community's goals.

Accept responsibility for shaping your own future.

Ask yourself regularly:

Am I living according to definitions I have chosen, or ones assigned by others?

True power begins with self-definition.

Conclusion

The laws within this book are not isolated ideas.

They form a framework.

A framework for understanding identity, navigating systems, building institutions, strengthening communities, and cultivating personal discipline.

When practiced together, these principles guide individuals toward a life of clarity, purpose, and constructive influence.

Power, in its highest form, is not domination.

It is the disciplined ability to determine one's direction and build a future aligned with one's values.

And that journey begins with a simple decision:

To define yourself—and to live accordingly.

Afterword

Why This Book Is Needed

Every generation inherits a world shaped by decisions it did not make.

Systems of power, economic structures, cultural expectations, and social institutions all existed long before any individual enters them. Many people therefore spend much of their lives reacting to circumstances rather than understanding the forces shaping those circumstances.

Without strategic awareness, individuals often move through life guided by assumptions rather than insight.

This book exists to challenge that condition.

It was written to provide readers with a framework for understanding power—not in the narrow sense of domination or control, but in the deeper sense of self-governance, strategic awareness, and disciplined decision-making.

Power in its highest form is the ability to understand the environment around you, define your identity clearly, and act with intention rather than confusion.

The modern world is complex. Institutions, technology, economic structures, and social systems influence opportunity in ways that are not always visible. Many individuals are taught how to work within these systems, but very few are taught how to analyze them strategically.

This book fills that gap.

The 48 Laws of Inner & Outer Righteous Power are designed to help readers develop clarity in three essential areas:

• Identity — understanding who you are and what principles guide you

• Strategy — learning how systems and institutions operate

• Discipline — developing habits that sustain long-term progress

Together these principles create a foundation for navigating life with greater awareness, responsibility, and purpose.

This book does not promise shortcuts or instant success.

Instead, it offers something more valuable:

a framework for disciplined thinking and strategic living.

Who This Book Is For

This book was written for individuals who are ready to think deeply about their lives and their environment.

It is for readers who want more than motivational slogans or temporary inspiration.

It is for those who seek understanding.

This manuscript may be especially useful for:

• Individuals seeking clarity about identity and personal direction

• Students and young professionals learning to navigate complex systems

• Community leaders and organizers developing long-term strategy

• Entrepreneurs and creators building independent paths

• Anyone interested in the study of power, discipline, and leadership

While the ideas within this book were inspired by real historical and social experiences, the principles themselves are universal.

They apply to individuals from many backgrounds who wish to develop stronger strategic awareness and personal discipline.

Ultimately, the ideal reader of this book is someone who understands that life is not merely something that happens to us.

It is something we must learn to navigate wisely.

Why This Book Matters Now

We live in an era of extraordinary information.

Technology allows knowledge to travel across the world instantly. Yet despite this abundance of information, many people struggle with confusion about identity, direction, and purpose.

Information alone does not produce clarity.

In many ways, modern life encourages distraction rather than reflection. Social media, constant news cycles, and endless streams of commentary often pull attention toward short-term reactions rather than long-term understanding.

As a result, many individuals spend their energy responding to events rather than developing a strategic vision for their lives.

This book encourages the opposite approach.

It invites readers to slow down, think carefully, and develop the habits that allow individuals and communities to build meaningful futures across decades rather than moments.

In a world that rewards speed and reaction, clarity and discipline become powerful advantages.

How to Use This Book Effectively

This book is not meant to be read once and placed on a shelf.

It is designed to function as a strategic manual.

Each of the 48 laws introduces a principle that can be studied, reflected upon, and applied repeatedly throughout life.

Readers may approach the book in several ways.

Sequential Reading

Reading the book from beginning to end provides a structured progression.

The early sections focus on personal mastery, including identity, emotional discipline, and mental clarity.

Later sections explore systems and institutions, followed by social relationships, economic strategy, and collective development.

The final section focuses on long-term leadership habits and self-determination.

Together these sections create a complete framework for understanding both inner and outer power.

Strategic Reference

Readers may also return to individual laws when facing specific challenges.

For example:

• periods of uncertainty may call for revisiting laws about identity and discipline

• professional challenges may benefit from laws concerning strategy and systems

• leadership roles may require reflection on laws about community and responsibility

Each law serves as a tool that can be applied repeatedly over time.

Reflection and Practice

At the end of every law is a Strategic Training Drill.

These exercises are not symbolic. They are intended to transform ideas into habits.

Powerful ideas only become meaningful when they are practiced consistently.

A Permanent Training Manual

The purpose of this manuscript is not merely to communicate ideas.

Its purpose is training.

Just as athletes strengthen their bodies through repeated practice, individuals strengthen their judgment and discipline through repeated reflection and action.

Over time, the principles in this book can become part of the reader's way of thinking.

They begin to influence decisions about identity, relationships, work, leadership, and long-term vision.

When this occurs, the book has served its true purpose.

It becomes not simply something that was read, but something that shapes the reader's approach to life.

Because the greatest form of power is not control over others.

It is the ability to govern oneself wisely and build a life aligned with purpose.

Closing Thought

The 48 laws presented in this manuscript do not claim to provide all answers.

Rather, they offer a framework for asking better questions.

Who am I?

What principles guide my decisions?

How do systems around me operate?

What future am I helping to build?

When individuals begin asking these questions with honesty and discipline, their lives often move in new directions.

Clarity replaces confusion.

Strategy replaces reaction.

Purpose replaces drift.

And from that transformation emerges something more powerful than influence or status.

It is the quiet confidence of a person who understands their identity, their environment, and their direction.

That is the foundation upon which true power is built.

If you'd like, I can also give you the next powerful page your book should include that will dramatically elevate it:

"The Philosophy of Righteous Power"

Every generation inherits a world shaped by decisions it did not make.

Systems of power, economic structures, cultural expectations, and social institutions all existed long before any individual enters them. Many people therefore spend much of their lives reacting to circumstances rather than understanding the forces shaping those circumstances.

Without strategic awareness, individuals often move through life guided by assumptions rather than insight.

This book exists to challenge that condition.

It was written to provide readers with a framework for understanding power—not in the narrow sense of domination or control, but in the deeper sense of self-governance, strategic awareness, and disciplined decision-making.

Power in its highest form is the ability to understand the environment around you, define your identity clearly, and act with intention rather than confusion.

The modern world is complex. Institutions, technology, economic structures, and social systems influence opportunity in ways that are not always visible. Many individuals are taught how to work within these systems, but very few are taught how to analyze them strategically.

This book fills that gap.

The 48 Laws of Inner & Outer Righteous Power are designed to help readers develop clarity in three essential areas:

• Identity — understanding who you are and what principles guide you

• Strategy — learning how systems and institutions operate

• Discipline — developing habits that sustain long-term progress

Together these principles create a foundation for navigating life with greater awareness, responsibility, and purpose.

This book does not promise shortcuts or instant success.

Instead, it offers something more valuable:

a framework for disciplined thinking and strategic living.

Who This Book Is For

This book was written for individuals who are ready to think deeply about their lives and their environment.

It is for readers who want more than motivational slogans or temporary inspiration.

It is for those who seek understanding.

This manuscript may be especially useful for:

• Individuals seeking clarity about identity and personal direction

• Students and young professionals learning to navigate complex systems

• Community leaders and organizers developing long-term strategy

• Entrepreneurs and creators building independent paths

• Anyone interested in the study of power, discipline, and leadership

While the ideas within this book were inspired by real historical and social experiences, the principles themselves are universal.

They apply to individuals from many backgrounds who wish to develop stronger strategic awareness and personal discipline.

Ultimately, the ideal reader of this book is someone who understands that life is not merely something that happens to us.

It is something we must learn to navigate wisely.

Why This Book Matters Now

We live in an era of extraordinary information.

Technology allows knowledge to travel across the world instantly. Yet despite this abundance of information, many people struggle with confusion about identity, direction, and purpose.

Information alone does not produce clarity.

In many ways, modern life encourages distraction rather than reflection. Social media, constant news cycles, and endless streams of commentary often pull attention toward short-term reactions rather than long-term understanding.

As a result, many individuals spend their energy responding to events rather than developing a strategic vision for their lives.

This book encourages the opposite approach.

It invites readers to slow down, think carefully, and develop the habits that allow individuals and communities to build meaningful futures across decades rather than moments.

In a world that rewards speed and reaction, clarity and discipline become powerful advantages.

How to Use This Book Effectively

This book is not meant to be read once and placed on a shelf.

It is designed to function as a strategic manual.

Each of the 48 laws introduces a principle that can be studied, reflected upon, and applied repeatedly throughout life.

Readers may approach the book in several ways.

Sequential Reading

Reading the book from beginning to end provides a structured progression.

The early sections focus on personal mastery, including identity, emotional discipline, and mental clarity.

Later sections explore systems and institutions, followed by social relationships, economic strategy, and collective development.

The final section focuses on long-term leadership habits and self-determination.

Together these sections create a complete framework for understanding both inner and outer power.

Strategic Reference

Readers may also return to individual laws when facing specific challenges.

For example:

• periods of uncertainty may call for revisiting laws about identity and discipline

• professional challenges may benefit from laws concerning strategy and systems

• leadership roles may require reflection on laws about community and responsibility

Each law serves as a tool that can be applied repeatedly over time.

Reflection and Practice

At the end of every law is a Strategic Training Drill.

These exercises are not symbolic. They are intended to transform ideas into habits.

Powerful ideas only become meaningful when they are practiced consistently.

A Permanent Training Manual

The purpose of this manuscript is not merely to communicate ideas.

Its purpose is training.

Just as athletes strengthen their bodies through repeated practice, individuals strengthen their judgment and discipline through repeated reflection and action.

Over time, the principles in this book can become part of the reader's way of thinking.

They begin to influence decisions about identity, relationships, work, leadership, and long-term vision.

When this occurs, the book has served its true purpose.

It becomes not simply something that was read, but something that shapes the reader's approach to life.

Because the greatest form of power is not control over others.

It is the ability to govern oneself wisely and build a life aligned with purpose.

Closing Thought

The 48 laws presented in this manuscript do not claim to provide all answers.

Rather, they offer a framework for asking better questions.

Who am I?

What principles guide my decisions?

How do systems around me operate?

What future am I helping to build?

When individuals begin asking these questions with honesty and discipline, their lives often move in new directions.

Clarity replaces confusion.

Strategy replaces reaction.

Purpose replaces drift.

And from that transformation emerges something more powerful than influence or status.

It is the quiet confidence of a person who understands their identity, their environment, and their direction.

That is the foundation upon which true power is built.

elevate it:

"The Philosophy of Righteous Power"

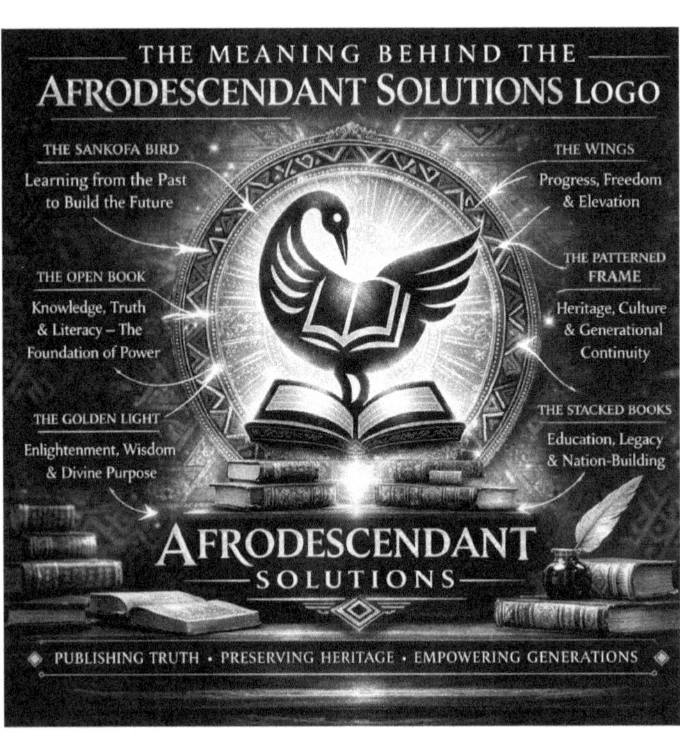
THE MEANING BEHIND THE
AFRODESCENDANT SOLUTIONS LOGO
THE SANKOFA BIRD
Learning from the Past to Build the Future
THE WINGS
Progress, Freedom & Elevation
THE OPEN BOOK
Knowledge, Truth & Literacy – The Foundation of Power
THE PATTERNED FRAME
Heritage, Culture & Generational Continuity
THE GOLDEN LIGHT
Enlightenment, Wisdom & Divine Purpose
THE STACKED BOOKS
Education, Legacy & Nation-Building
AFRODESCENDANT
SOLUTIONS
PUBLISHING TRUTH • PRESERVING HERITAGE • EMPOWERING GENERATIONS

www.ingramcontent.com/pod-product-compliance
Lightning Source LLC
LaVergne TN
LVHW010651110826
845149LV00014B/3031

9781972094044